SERVING AT SATAN'S ALTAR

The Satanic Truth About God, Satan, and The Left Hand Path

W.L. NEWTON

Copyright © 2020 by W.L. Newton.

ISBN:	Hardcover	978-1-6641-3122-4
	Softcover	978-1-6641-3123-1
	eBook	978-1-6641-3121-7

All rights reserved. No part of this book may be reproduced or transmitted in any form or by any means, electronic or mechanical, including photocopying, recording, or by any information storage and retrieval system, without permission in writing from the copyright owner.

Any people depicted in stock imagery provided by Getty Images are models, and such images are being used for illustrative purposes only.
Certain stock imagery © Getty Images.

Unless otherwise indicated, all scripture quotations are from The Holy Bible, English Standard Version® (ESV®). Copyright ©2001 by Crossway Bibles, a division of Good News Publishers. Used by permission. All rights reserved.

Print information available on the last page.

Rev. date: 09/15/2020

To order additional copies of this book, contact:
Xlibris
844-714-8691
www.Xlibris.com
Orders@Xlibris.com
819619

CONTENTS

Introduction vii

Chapter 1 1
Chapter 2 48
Chapter 3 51
Chapter 4 56
Chapter 5 59
Chapter 6 62
Chapter 7 66
Chapter 8 68
Chapter 9 94
Chapter 10 102
Chapter 11 105

INTRODUCTION

The world is not what you think it is, the life you live is not living in the true since of the word. Lies, Lies, Lies!!!! Yet we get up every morning thinking of this being called God, and we think to ourselves that he has everything under control, that in the end all will be made right and justice will be served. This is the greatest of all lies!

Nothing could be farther from the truth. This God is the very entity that will drive mankind to its ultimate end, Armageddon! We are told this numerous times throughout the so-called holy book of the bible. Yet we haven't the foggiest idea of what is really going on. Why? Our religions as well as governments, institutions of all types have pulled the wool over our eyes and have kept the truth from us. Yes, this God is leading us, but to what? Is it the ultimate salvation in a heaven or paradise? Or could it be something else, something a hell of a lot more sinister?

CHAPTER 1

I remember as a child, waking up and the first thing I would do is pray to god to keep me safe as well as the safety of my family, and to be with us and forgive anything we might do wrong so that he would still love us. I did this all the time, even at bed time. I read the bible, went to church, and just wanted nothing but this god's love. He is all I ever wanted. I wanted to serve him as a priest, which I actually did. I loved being a priest and serving this god through the people. I didn't care about money, for the love of money was evil. If I was poor, it was okay, for this was god's will. No matter what happened it was his will. He had everything under control and it was all for my own good, as well as the good of all others who loved him.

It was a way of living for me, a way where god took care of everything, no matter the choice I made, for it was his will that would happen. He led all of those who believed and loved him. No matter the circumstances, no matter the problems in life, it was all for me and for my good for god loved me, he gave his only son for me!

We have all heard this since our earliest days, so it's nothing new. I would walk around being called father, and yes, I loved that as well, for I could even forgive the sins of those who would confess their sins to me, this is a good deal I would think. God has invested me with power to heal, forgive, expel unwanted demons and to bless all those I felt worthy, wow! A lot of power and responsibility for a man.

This is the beginning of sorrows though; I didn't realize this at the time. Yet when the truth actually hits you, it's not fun to see the real picture, the true script written and yet kept from all of us except those who are in the know, the so-called elite! They know what is really happening, the truth behind all of it. I soon became one of those who knew the truth, and it doesn't set you free....it sends you deeper into the prison of lies!

We are all taught that the bible is the word of god, and it is perfect. Let me show you its perfection.

The bible claims that it is gods very word and that god himself has given this to holy men as they were moved by the holy spirit/2 Peter 1:21

Yet the very god who had inspired this verse says this in Jeremiah:

The prophets prophesy lies in my name. /Jer 23:25

How could this be? This is a flat-out contradiction! But this is just the tip of the iceberg. There is so much more then this as you will see. For Jeremiah also says this:

The false pen of the scribes hath wrought falsely/Jer 8:8

So here again we see that this god who supposedly inspired all of these verses is saying flat out that these men who are called holy have lied and changed everything. Wow! What a confusing mess this is getting to be.

Even the new testament is full of things like this. Such as John, he is recorded say this as well as other things that do not exactly matchup. This is what he has said of Jesus,

He that saw it bare record and his record is true, and he knoweth that he sayeth true, that ye might believe/John 19:35 Then this Jesus says this:

I have greater witness then John, though I bare record of myself, yet my record is true. /John 8:14

Read this carefully, he says that he can bare record of himself and it is true, but in chapter 5 he said this:

If I bare witness of myself, my witness is not true. /John 5:31

How can both be true? It can't be, only one can be true, period!

Yet again let's look to another, in fact let's look to Paul who wrote more of the new testament then anyone, in fact he is the one quoted more often than any of the disciples, those who actually lived with this Jesus. Paul says this:

I speak the truth in Christ, I lie not, my conscience also bearing me witness in the Holy Ghost/Rom 9:1

Here Paul lets us know that it is through the witness of the Holy Ghost that he lies not, really????? Let's look just 6 chapters before this and see what Paul says.

For if the truth of god hath more abounded through my LIE unto his glory, why yet am I also judged a sinner. /Rom 3:7

I ask again, how can this be? In chapter 3 Paul says he lies for the glory of god, and in chapter 9 he says that even the holy ghost along with his conscience proves he does not lie. A pure contradiction wouldn't you say? Jesus proclaims in John 18:36 that his kingdom is not of this world, Jesus also claimed that the world hated him because he testified that the works of it were evil, John 7:7, also that if the world hates you, know it hated him first, John 15:18, That the world loves its own, John 15:19, he has given the world the word of the Father and it hates him for it, John 17:14, marvel not that the world hates you,1John :13, all of this world hates you and him and god, yet with all of this said, Jesus says this:

There is no man that hath left house, or brethren, sisters or father, mother, or wife, or children or lands, for my sake and the gospels, but he shall receive 100 fold NOW in THIS TIME, houses and brethren, sisters, mothers and children and lands with persecutions and in the world to come, eternal life/Mark 10:29-30.

With all of the hatred of this world going to all who love this Jesus as well as Jesus himself, and seeing that he and his kingdom are not of this world, yet to give up your family and property for him and his gospel will increase your worldly wealth 100-fold! So, hate the world, hate money, yet you will be given 100-fold more then you gave up in this world, in the very time you do this act of love towards him. How many people have done this through the ages and wound up homeless and still hated for his name sake? How many christians were killed after they had given up everything for Jesus and the gospel yet where was this 100-fold blessing in this life???? Where???!!!!

I know of no christian who was saved from the Romans, or anyone else. I know of no one who was saved from the burnings committed by the christians on the so-called heathens either. It just does not happen so this was a massive lie! Do you see where I'm going with all of this. How can this be the inspired word of god and yet it is full of people who not only contradict themselves, but come out and admit they are lying! It gets worse though.

This religion called christianity now tells their adherents that they must watch and pray always, and they must give up their property and all they have, just as Jesus told them to do, yet they are not to be rewarded 100 fold, in fact they are actually scammed and punished for not doing so. In the book of acts we are given the story of Ananias and his wife Sapphira. In this story this couple sells their lands and decides to keep some of the money, so first the husband Ananias gives the money to the disciples and doesn't tell them the true price of the land, so he is struck down dead at once, and then the wife come to them hours later and she herself is struck down dead. Why? Because the decided to give only a portion of the money, and now they paid with their lives! The church needed the money more, I guess. What this does is strike fear into the hearts of believers so they won't keep any of the money for themselves, for the church leaders are apparently much more powerful for they have the Holy Spirit with them and this gives them the power over even life and death of the congregations.

This new religion which actually has done nothing new, for it stole everything from pagan religions, now took the Gods and changed it into a One God religion, yet this one god is one in three, which makes no sense in itself. Even the catholic church admits this in vol 15 of the catholic encyclopedia, that:

not only did they take the pagan gods and change them into saints, but that the saints are the successors to the gods!

If christians would do their studies, they would find the terrible truth that all of their so-called pious observances, prayers, hymns, baptism, alters, communions, redemption, salvation, along with all of their holy days such as Christmas and Easter with of course the resurrection, all of them are from pagan practices that are thousands of years older than this religion. Even Jesus is just another in a long line of saviors who die and resurrect again for the people. Need I say any more? Yet I must!

If this isn't good enough for you, lets go through the bible and see what it actually says. We are told we are slaves; we are told about how this god loves murder, rape, genocide! After reading these verses, you tell me if this is the god of truth, or if this religion is for real people or for those who want to keep us as slaves!

Colossians 4:1 ESV /

Masters, treat your slaves justly and fairly, knowing that you also have a Master in heaven.

Exodus 21:16 ESV /

"Whoever steals a man and sells him, and anyone found in possession of him, shall be put to death.

Ephesians 6:5 ESV /

Slaves, obey your earthly masters with fear and trembling, with a sincere heart, as you would Christ,

Leviticus 25:44-46 ESV /

As for your male and female slaves whom you may have: you may buy male and female slaves from among the nations that are around you. You may also buy from among the strangers who sojourn with you and their clans that are with you, who have been born in your land, and they may be your property. You may bequeath them to your sons after you to inherit as a possession forever. You may make slaves of them, but over your brothers the people of Israel you shall not rule, one over another ruthlessly.

Exodus 21:20-21 ESV /

"When a man strikes his slave, male or female, with a rod and the slave dies under his hand, he shall be avenged. But if the slave survives a day or two, he is not to be avenged, for the slave is his money.

Galatians 5:1 ESV /

For freedom Christ has set us free; stand firm therefore, and do not submit again to a yoke of slavery.

Galatians 3:28 ESV /

There is neither Jew nor Greek, there is neither slave nor free, there is no male and female, for you are all one in Christ Jesus.

1 Peter 2:18 ESV

Servants, be subject to your masters with all respect, not only to the good and gentle but also to the unjust.

Philemon 1:16 ESV /

No longer as a slave but more than a slave, as a beloved brother—especially to me, but how much more to you, both in the flesh and in the Lord.

Titus 2:9-10 ESV /

Slaves are to be submissive to their own masters in everything; they are to be well-pleasing, not argumentative, not pilfering, but showing all good faith, so that in everything they may adorn the doctrine of God our Savior.

Exodus 21:26-27 ESV

"When a man strikes the eye of his slave, male or female, and destroys it, he shall let the slave go free because of his eye. If he knocks out the tooth of his slave, male or female, he shall let the slave go free because of his tooth.

Ephesians 6:9 ESV /

Masters, do the same to them, and stop your threatening, knowing that he who is both their Master and yours is in heaven, and that there is no partiality with him.

Luke 4:18 ESV /

"The Spirit of the Lord is upon me, because he has anointed me to proclaim good news to the poor. He has sent me to proclaim liberty to the captives and recovering of sight to the blind, to set at liberty those who are oppressed,

1 Timothy 6:1 ESV /

Let all who are under a yoke as slaves regard their own masters as worthy of all honor, so that the name of God and the teaching may not be reviled.

Exodus 21:2 ESV /

When you buy a Hebrew slave, he shall serve six years, and in the seventh he shall go out free, for nothing.

Deuteronomy 24:7 ESV /

"If a man is found stealing one of his brothers of the people of Israel, and if he treats him as a slave or sells him, then that thief shall die. So, you shall purge the evil from your midst.

1 Timothy 6:1-2 ESV /

Let all who are under a yoke as slaves regard their own masters as worthy of all honor, so that the name of God and the teaching may not be reviled. Those who have believing masters must not be disrespectful on the ground that they are brothers; rather they must serve all the better since those who benefit by their good service are believers and beloved. Teach and urge these things.

1 Peter 2:16 ESV /

Live as people who are free, not using your freedom as a cover-up for evil, but living as servants of God.

Exodus 21:1-36 ESV /

"Now these are the rules that you shall set before them. When you buy a Hebrew slave, he shall serve six years, and in the seventh he shall go out free, for nothing. If he comes in single, he shall go out single; if he comes in married, then his wife shall go out with him. If his master gives him a wife and she bear him sons or daughters, the wife and her children shall be her master's, and he shall go out alone. But if the slave plainly says, 'I love my master, my wife, and my children; I will not go out free,' ...

Deuteronomy 23:15 ESV /

"You shall not give up to his master a slave who has escaped from his master to you.

1 Timothy 1:10 ESV

The sexually immoral, men who practice homosexuality, enslavers, liars, perjurers, and whatever else is contrary to sound doctrine,

Colossians 3:22 ESV

Slaves, obey in everything those who are your earthly masters, not by way of eye-service, as people-pleasers, but with sincerity of heart, fearing the Lord.

Exodus 21:2-6 ESV

When you buy a Hebrew slave, he shall serve six years, and in the seventh he shall go out free, for nothing. If he comes in single, he shall go out single; if he comes in married, then his wife shall go out with him. If his master gives him a wife and she bear him sons or daughters, the wife and her children shall be her master's, and he shall go out alone. But if the slave plainly says, 'I love my master, my wife, and my children; I will not go out free,' then his master shall bring him to God, and he shall bring him to the door or the doorpost. And his master shall bore his ear through with an awl, and he shall be his slave forever.

Ephesians 6:5-8 ESV /

Slaves, obey your earthly masters with fear and trembling, with a sincere heart, as you would Christ, not by the way of eye-service, as people-pleasers, but as servants of Christ, doing the will of God from the heart, rendering service with a good will as to the Lord and not to man, knowing that whatever good anyone does, this he will receive back from the Lord, whether he is a slave or free.

Luke 12:47-48 ESV

And that servant who knew his master's will but did not get ready or act according to his will, will receive a severe beating. But the one who did not know, and did what deserved a beating, will receive a light beating. Everyone to whom much was given, of him much will be required, and from him to whom they entrusted much, they will demand the more.

1 Corinthians 7:21 ESV

Were you a slave when called? Do not be concerned about it. (But if you can gain your freedom, avail yourself of the opportunity.)

Exodus 21:7 ESV

"When a man sells his daughter as a slave, she shall not go out as the male slaves do.

Exodus 21:32 ESV /

If the ox gores a slave, male or female, the owner shall give to their master thirty shekels of silver, and the ox shall be stoned.

Leviticus 25:1-55 ESV /

The Lord spoke to Moses on Mount Sinai, saying, "Speak to the people of Israel and say to them, when you come into the land that I give you, the land shall keep a Sabbath to the Lord. For six years you shall sow your field, and for six years you shall prune your vineyard and gather in its fruits, but in the seventh year there shall be a Sabbath of solemn rest for the land, a Sabbath to the Lord. You shall not sow your field or prune your vineyard. You shall not reap what grows of itself in your harvest, or gather the grapes of your undressed vine. It shall be a year of solemn rest for the land. ...

Ephesians 6:5-9 ESV /

Slaves, obey your earthly masters with fear and trembling, with a sincere heart, as you would Christ, not by the way of eye-service, as people-pleasers, but as servants of Christ, doing the will of God from the heart, rendering service with a good will as to the Lord and not to man, knowing that whatever good anyone does, this he will receive back from the Lord, whether he is a slave or free. Masters, do the same to them, and stop your threatening, knowing that he who is both their Master and yours is in heaven, and that there is no partiality with him.

John 8:34 ESV

Jesus answered them, "Truly, truly, I say to you, everyone who commits sin is a slave to sin.

Exodus 21:20 ESV

"When a man strikes his slave, male or female, with a rod and the slave dies under his hand, he shall be avenged.

Deuteronomy 5:15 ESV

You shall remember that you were a slave in the land of Egypt, and the Lord your God brought you out from there with a mighty hand and an outstretched arm. Therefore, the Lord your God commanded you to keep the Sabbath day.

Proverbs 22:16

Whoever oppresses the poor to increase his own wealth, or gives to the rich, will only come to poverty.

Romans 1:1 ESV

Paul, a servant of Christ Jesus, called to be an apostle, set apart for the gospel of God,

Exodus 21:7-11 ESV

"When a man sells his daughter as a slave, she shall not go out as the male slaves do. If she does not please her master, who has designated her for himself, then he shall let her be redeemed. He shall have no right to sell her to a foreign people, since he has broken faith with her. If he designates her for his son, he shall deal with her as with a daughter. If he takes another wife to himself, he shall not diminish her food, her clothing, or her marital rights. And if he does not do these three things for her, she shall go out for nothing, without payment of money.

1 Corinthians 12:13 ESV

For in one Spirit we were all baptized into one body—Jews or Greeks, slaves or free—and all were made to drink of one Spirit.

Proverbs 12:24 ESV

The hand of the diligent will rules, while the slothful will be put to forced labor.

Romans 8:15 ESV

For you did not receive the spirit of slavery to fall back into fear, but you have received the Spirit of adoption as sons, by whom we cry, "Abba! Father!"

Leviticus 25:44 ESV /

As for your male and female slaves whom you may have: you may buy male and female slaves from among the nations that are around you.

Romans 6:22 ESV /

But now that you have been set free from sin and have become slaves of God, the fruit you get leads to sanctification and its end, eternal life.

Acts 17:26 ESV /

And he made from one man every nation of mankind to live on all the face of the earth, having determined allotted periods and the boundaries of their dwelling place,

Deuteronomy 15:12 ESV /

"If your brother, a Hebrew man or a Hebrew woman, is sold to you, he shall serve you six years, and in the seventh year you shall let him go free from you.

Deuteronomy 15:12-18 ESV /

"If your brother, a Hebrew man or a Hebrew woman, is sold to you, he shall serve you six years, and in the seventh year you shall let him go free from you. And when you let him go free from you, you shall not let him go empty-handed. You shall furnish him liberally out of your flock, out of your threshing floor, and out of your winepress. As the Lord your God has blessed you, you shall give to him. You shall remember that you were a slave in the land of Egypt, and the Lord your God redeemed you; therefore, I command you this today. But if he says to you, 'I will not go out from you,' because he loves you and your household, since he is well-off with you, ...

Leviticus 25:39 ESV /

"If your brother becomes poor beside you and sells himself to you, you shall not make him serve as a slave:

John 8:36 ESV / 1,127 helpful votes

So, if the Son sets you free, you will be free indeed.

1 Corinthians 7:21-23 ESV /

Were you a slave when called? Do not be concerned about it. (But if you can gain your freedom, avail yourself of the opportunity.) For he who was called in the Lord as a slave is a freedman of the Lord. Likewise, he who was free when called is a slave of Christ. You were bought with a price; do not become slaves of men.

Genesis 9:25 ESV /

He said, "Cursed be Canaan; a servant of servants shall he be to his brothers."

Deuteronomy 15:12-15 ESV /

"If your brother, a Hebrew man or a Hebrew woman, is sold to you, he shall serve you six years, and in the seventh year you shall let him go free from you. And when you let him go free from you, you shall not let him go empty-handed. You shall furnish him liberally out of your flock, out of your threshing floor, and out of your winepress. As the Lord your God has blessed you, you shall give to him. You shall remember that you were a slave in the land of Egypt, and the Lord your God redeemed you; therefore, I command you this today.

Leviticus 25:43 ESV

You shall not rule over him ruthlessly but shall fear your God.

Isaiah 58:6 ESV

"Is not this the fast that I choose: to lose the bonds of wickedness, to undo the straps of the yoke, to let the oppressed go free, and to break every yoke?

Proverbs 22:7 ESV /

The rich rules over the poor, and the borrower is the slave of the lender.

Titus 2:9 ESV /

Slaves are to be submissive to their own masters in everything; they are to be well-pleasing, not argumentative,

Exodus 21:18-21 ESV

"When men quarrel and one strikes the other with a stone or with his fist and the man does not die but takes to his bed, then if the man rises again and walks outdoors with his staff, he who struck him shall be clear; only he shall pay for the loss of his time, and shall have him thoroughly healed. "When a man strikes his slave, male or female, with a rod and the slave dies under his hand, he shall be avenged. But if the slave survives a day or two, he is not to be avenged, for the slave is his money.

Exodus 20:1-26 ESV

And God spoke all these words, saying, "I am the Lord your God, who brought you out of the land of Egypt, out of the house of slavery. "You shall have no other gods before me. "You shall not make for yourself a carved image, or any likeness of anything that is in heaven above, or that is in the earth beneath, or that is in the water under the earth. You shall not bow down to them or serve them, for I the Lord your God am a jealous God, visiting the iniquity of the fathers on the children to the third and the fourth generation of those who hate me, ...

Exodus 21:12 ESV /

"Whoever strikes a man so that he dies shall be put to death.

Genesis 1:27 ESV

So, God created man in his own image, in the image of God he created him; male and female he created them.

Genesis 15:13-14 ESV

Then the Lord said to Abram, "Know for certain that your offspring will be sojourners in a land that is not theirs and will be servants there, and they will be afflicted for four hundred years. But I will bring judgment on the nation that they serve, and afterward they shall come out with great possessions.

Matthew 25:46 ESV /

And these will go away into eternal punishment, but the righteous into eternal life."

Exodus 21:4 ESV

If his master gives him a wife and she bear him sons or daughters, the wife and her children shall be her master's, and he shall go out alone.

Luke 16:13 Esv

No servant can serve two masters, for either he will hate the one and love the other, or he will be devoted to the one and despise the other. You cannot serve God and money."

Luke 12:43-48 ESv

Blessed is that servant whom his master will find so doing when he comes. Truly, I say to you, he will set him over all his possessions. But if that servant says to himself, 'My master is delayed in coming,' and begins to beat the male and female servants, and to eat and drink and get drunk, the master of that servant will come on a day when he does not expect him and at an hour he does not know, and will cut him in pieces and put him with the unfaithful. And that servant who knew his master's will but did not get ready or act according to his will, will receive a severe beating. ...

Exodus 21:8 ESV

If she does not please her master, who has designated her for himself, then he shall let her be redeemed. He shall have no right to sell her to a foreign people, since he has broken faith with her.

Romans 6:5-6 ESV /

For if we have been united with him in a death like his, we shall certainly be united with him in a resurrection like his. We know that our old self was crucified with him in order that the body of sin might be brought to nothing, so that we would no longer be enslaved to sin.

Deuteronomy 21:10-14 ESV

"When you go out to war against your enemies, and the Lord your God gives them into your hand and you take them captive, and you see among the captives a beautiful woman, and you desire to take her to be your wife, and you bring her home to your house, she shall shave her head and pare her nails. And she shall take off the clothes in which she was captured and shall remain in your house and lament her father and her mother a full month. After that you may go in to her and be her husband, and she shall be your wife. But if you no longer delight in her, you shall let her go where she wants. But you shall not sell her for money, nor shall you treat her as a slave, since you have humiliated her.

Galatians 3:28-29 ESV /

There is neither Jew nor Greek, there is neither slave nor free, there is no male and female, for you are all one in Christ Jesus. And if you are Christ's, then you are Abraham's offspring, heirs according to promise.

Leviticus 25:38-46 ESV /

I am the Lord your God, who brought you out of the land of Egypt to give you the land of Canaan, and to be your God. "If your brother becomes poor beside you and sells himself to you, you shall not make him serve as a slave: he shall be with you as a hired servant and as a sojourner. He shall serve with you until the year of the jubilee. Then he shall go out from you, he and his children with him, and go back to his own clan and return to the possession of his fathers. For they are my servants, whom I brought out of the land of Egypt; they shall not be sold as slaves. ...

Leviticus 19:20 ESV /

"If a man lies sexually with a woman who is a slave, assigned to another man and not yet ransomed or given her freedom, a distinction shall be made. They shall not be put to death, because she was not free;

Deuteronomy 23:15-16 ESV /

"You shall not give up to his master a slave who has escaped from his master to you. He shall dwell with you, in your midst, in the place that he shall choose within one of your towns, wherever it suits him. You shall not wrong him.

Exodus 3:1-15:27 ESV

Now Moses was keeping the flock of his father-in-law, Jethro, the priest of Midian, and he led his flock to the west side of the wilderness and came to Horeb, the mountain of God. And the angel of the Lord appeared to him in a flame of fire out of the midst of a bush. He looked, and behold, the bush was burning, yet it was not consumed. And Moses said, "I will turn aside to see this great sight, why the bush is not burned." When the Lord saw that he turned aside to see, God called to him out of the bush, "Moses, Moses!" And he said, "Here I am." Then he said, "Do not come near; take your sandals off your feet, for the place on which you are standing is holy ground." ...

Genesis 4:1-26 ESV /

Now Adam knew Eve his wife, and she conceived and bore Cain, saying, "I have gotten a man with the help of the Lord." And again, she bore his brother Abel. Now Abel was a keeper of sheep, and Cain a worker of the ground. In the course of time Cain brought to the Lord an offering of the fruit of the ground, and Abel also brought of the firstborn of his flock and of their fat portions. And the Lord had regard for Abel and his offering, but for Cain and his offering he had no regard. So, Cain was very angry, and his face fell. ...

Leviticus 19:20-22 ESV /

"If a man lies sexually with a woman who is a slave, assigned to another man and not yet ransomed or given her freedom, a distinction shall be made. They shall not be put to death, because she was not free; but he shall bring his compensation to the Lord, to the entrance of the tent of meeting, a ram for a guilt offering. And the priest shall make atonement for him with the ram of the guilt offering before the Lord for his sin that he has committed, and he shall be forgiven for the sin that he has committed.

1 Timothy 1:9-10 ESV /

Understanding this, that the law is not laid down for the just but for the lawless and disobedient, for the ungodly and sinners, for the unholy and profane, for those who strike their fathers and mothers, for murderers, the sexually immoral, men who practice homosexuality, enslavers, liars, perjurers, and whatever else is contrary to sound doctrine,

Leviticus 25:46 ESV /

You may bequeath them to your sons after you to inherit as a possession forever. You may make slaves of them, but over your brothers the people of Israel you shall not rule, one over another ruthlessly.

Matthew 6:24 ESV /

"No one can serve two masters, for either he will hate the one and love the other, or he will be devoted to the one and despise the other. You cannot serve God and money.

Leviticus 25:53 ESV /

He shall treat him as a servant hired year by year. He shall not rule ruthlessly over him in your sight.

Genesis 11:1-32 ESV /

Now the whole earth had one language and the same words. And as people migrated from the east, they found a plain in the land of Shinar and settled there. And they said to one another, "Come, let us make bricks, and burn them thoroughly." And they had brick for stone, and bitumen for mortar. Then they said, "Come, let us build ourselves a city and a tower with its top in the heavens, and let us make a name for ourselves, lest we be dispersed over the face of the whole earth." And the Lord came down to see the city and the tower, which the children of man had built. ...

Romans 1:30 ESV /

Slanderers, haters of God, insolent, haughty, boastful, inventors of evil, disobedient to parents,

Deuteronomy 15:16-17 ESV /

But if he says to you, 'I will not go out from you,' because he loves you and your household, since he is well-off with you, then you shall take an awl, and put it through his ear into the door, and he shall be your slave forever. And to your female slave you shall do the same.

Leviticus 19:33-34 ESV /

"When a stranger sojourn with you in your land, you shall not do him wrong. You shall treat the stranger who sojourns with you as the native among you, and you shall love him as yourself, for you were strangers in the land of Egypt: I am the Lord your God.

Exodus 22:3 ESV /

But if the sun has risen on him, there shall be bloodguilt for him. He shall surely pay. If he has nothing, then he shall be sold for his theft.

Ephesians 6:6 ESV /

Not by the way of eye-service, as people-pleasers, but as servants of Christ, doing the will of God from the heart,

Jeremiah 34:14 ESV /

'At the end of seven years each of you must set free the fellow Hebrew who has been sold to you and has served you six years; you must set him free from your service.' But your fathers did not listen to me or incline their ears to me.

Deuteronomy 20:14 ESV /

But the women and the little ones, the livestock, and everything else in the city, all its spoil, you shall take as plunder for yourselves. And you shall enjoy the spoil of your enemies, which the Lord your God has given you.

Exodus 22:2-3 ESV /

If a thief is found breaking in and is struck so that he dies, there shall be no bloodguilt for him, but if the sun has risen on him, there shall be bloodguilt for him. He shall surely pay. If he has nothing, then he shall be sold for his theft.

Deuteronomy 13:5 ESV /

But that prophet or that dreamer of dreams shall be put to death, because he has taught rebellion against the Lord your God, who brought you out of the land of Egypt and redeemed you out of the house of slavery, to make you leave the way in which the Lord your God commanded you to walk. So, you shall purge the evil from your midst.

Matthew 10:24 ESV /

"A disciple is not above his teacher, nor a servant above his master.

Colossians 3:12 ESV /

Put on then, as God's chosen ones, holy and beloved, compassionate hearts, kindness, humility, meekness, and patience,

Exodus 21:6 ESV /

Then his master shall bring him to God, and he shall bring him to the door or the doorpost. And his master shall bore his ear through with an awl, and he shall be his slave forever.

Exodus 21:1 ESV /

"Now these are the rules that you shall set before them.

Colossians 3:22-24 ESV /

Slaves, obey in everything those who are your earthly masters, not by way of eye-service, as people-pleasers, but with sincerity of heart, fearing the Lord. Whatever you do, work heartily, as for the Lord and not for men, knowing that from the Lord you will receive the inheritance as your reward. You are serving the Lord Christ.

Exodus 20:10 ESV /

But the seventh day is a Sabbath to the Lord your God. On it you shall not do any work, you, or your son, or your daughter, your male servant, or your female servant, or your livestock, or the sojourner who is within your gates.

Colossians 3:11 ESV /

Here there is not Greek and Jew, circumcised and uncircumcised, barbarian, Scythian, slave, free; but Christ is all, and in all.

Jeremiah 34:9 ESV

That everyone should set free his Hebrew slaves, male and female, so that no one should enslave a Jew, his brother.

Revelation 1:1-20 ESV /

The revelation of Jesus Christ, which God gave him to show to his servants the things that must soon take place. He made it known by sending his angel to his servant John, who bore witness to the word of God and to the testimony of Jesus Christ, even to all that he saw. Blessed is the one who reads aloud the words of this prophecy, and blessed are those who hear, and who keep what is written in it, for the time is near. John to the seven churches that are in Asia: Grace to you and peace from him who is and who was and who is to come, and from the seven spirits who are before his throne, and from Jesus Christ the faithful witness, the firstborn of the dead, and the ruler of kings on earth. To him who loves us and has freed us from our sins by his blood ...

Exodus 21:1-4 ESV /

"Now these are the rules that you shall set before them. When you buy a Hebrew slave, he shall serve six years, and in the seventh he shall go out free, for nothing. If he comes in single, he shall go out single; if he comes in married, then his wife shall go out with him. If his master gives him a wife and she bear him sons or daughters, the wife and her children shall be her master's, and he shall go out alone.

Luke 7:1-10 ESV /

After he had finished all his sayings in the hearing of the people, he entered Capernaum. Now a centurion had a servant who was sick and at the point of death, who was highly valued by him. When the centurion heard about Jesus, he sent to him elders of the Jews, asking him to come and heal his servant. And when they came to Jesus, they pleaded with him earnestly, saying, "He is worthy to have you do this for him, for he loves our nation, and he is the one who built us our synagogue." ...

1 Corinthians 6:12 ESV /

"All things are lawful for me," but not all things are helpful. "All things are lawful for me," but I will not be enslaved by anything.

Exodus 21:11 ESV

And if he does not do these three things for her, she shall go out for nothing, without payment of money.

Deuteronomy 15:18 ESV

It shall not seem hard to you when you let him go free from you, for at half the cost of a hired servant he has served you six years. So, the Lord your God will bless you in all that you do.

Now let's look at the prophecies that Christians use to prove Jesus as the Messiah. Once read, I have no idea how this can be considered as valid for proof of his messiahship! not the last who arose to proclaim himself the Messiah or Christ.

This Jesus himself declared: "For many shall come hi my name, saying I am Christ; and shall deceive many. . .. Then if any man shall say, Lo, here is Christ, or there, believe it not. For there shall arise false Christs, and shall show great signs and wonders; insomuch that, if it were possible, they shall deceive the very elect" (Matt, xxiv, 5, 2324; Mark xiii, 6, 2122). And the intervening verses between those cited, are filled with a long catalogue of "great signs and wonders" which these Pretenders shall work in proof of them false claims.

How and why these false Pretenders to Messiahship could "come in my name" in the name of Yahveh's genuine Messiah, who had already come and by his own "signs and wonders" had demonstrated to the satisfaction of all who believed them, that he thus "fulfilled all the law and the prophets" and was indeed the Messiah and thus closed the lists, is not at this day very evident. But, admittedly, the working of such "great signs and wonders" miracles was no authentic badge of Messiahship, but was the common stock in trade of any bogus Pretender. Of this fact there are many Scriptural assurances and instances, besides the admission just made by Jesus. A very curious instance of Pretended Messiahship noted in the New Testament, was Simon Magnus, the Sorcerer, who notoriously "used sorcery, and bewitched the* people of Samaria, from the least to the greatest," so that all the people said, "This man is the great power of God," and "of a long time he had bewitched them with sorceries" (Acts viii, 9-11), which seems a very silly superstition to be vouched for by the Bible, and does not much credit to its inspired truth. The case of Elymas Bar-Jesus is also somewhat in point (Acts xiii, 6,

8); as is also that of the "damsel possessed with a spirit of divination, which brought her masters much gain by soothsaying" (Acts xvi, 16), or common fortune-telling. And even greater "signs and wonders" were worked by common charlatans.

Thus, even total strangers to Jesus Christ, uncommission by him, disbelievers in him, common Fakirs and false Pretenders, could exercise the divine power of "casting out devils" in his name, to the great scandal of the Disciples (Mark ix, 38; Luke ix, 49).

Yet all these miraculous powers, these "great signs and wonders," were clearly not of God, and prove no divine mission or authority of the wonder-workers: although Nicodemus declares, "No man can do these miracles that thou doest except God be with him" (Jn. iii, 2). Howbeit, Jesus himself appealed to this very power of working "signs and wonders" as the culminating proof and Patent of his divine authority and Messiahship: "For the same works that I do, bear witness of me, that the Father hath sent me" (Jn. v, 36); and, "though ye believe me not, believe the works" (Jn. x, 38); and again, "Believe me for the very works' sake" (Jn. xiv, 11).

But such "works," such "great signs and wonders," are proven by Bible proofs to prove nothing as Jesus himself had just averred and admitted except great credulity of people to believe them.

The proof of the divine mission and authority of Jesus as the Christ must, therefore, derive from some more valid evidences than that of mere popular wonder-working: though Jesus himself considered his "signs and wonders" as greater and more persuasive proof than the inspired assurances of his only human witnesses, the Gospel writers: "But I receive not testimony from man. . .. But I have greater witness than John; for . . . the same works that I do, bear witness of me, that the Father hath sent me" (Jn. v, 34, 36). And Jesus himself wholly discounts his own claims for himself, for he declares: "If I bear witness of myself, my witness is not true" (Jn. v, 31).

Therefore, with the testimony of "man," John and other Gospel biographers discounted; with his own testimony for himself declared "not true"; with the "witness of the works" discredited as being the common arts of charlatans and false Pretenders, we must need, in seeking proofs and satisfying evidences of the truth of claims that Jesus Christ is the true "Promised Messiah" of the Hebrew Prophets, turn to and examine these "prophecies," and the "internal evidences" of the Gospels, if haply they may prove themselves worthy of the high credit of truth.

1. THE MIRACULOUS "VIRGIN BIRTH" OF JESUS

Matthew, whose Gospel was written later, comes first in the order of Gospels in our printed collections, rather naturally for the reason that he gives a detailed "revelation" of the manner of miraculous conception and virgin-birth of the Subject of his inspired Biography.

He begins his Book with the genealogy of Jesus, which we elsewhere take notice of. He then proceeds with inspired pen to record: "Now the birth of Jesus Christ was on this wise: When his mother Mary was espoused to Joseph, before they came together, she was found with child of the Holy Ghost (v. 18). Then Joseph her husband, being a just man, and not willing to make her a public example, was minded to put her away privily (v. 19). But while he thought on these things, behold, the angel of Yahveh appeared unto him in a dream, saying, Joseph, thou son of David, fear not to take unto thee Mary thy wife: for that which is conceived in her is of the Holy Ghost (v. 20). (21)

THE "PROPHECIES" OF JESUS CHRIST 283

And she shall bring forth a son, and thou shall call his name Jesus: for he shall save his people from their sins." The foregoing is pure Fiction; here follows the crowning instance wherein "the false pen of the Scribes hath wrought falsely" (22) "Now all this was done, that it might be fulfilled which was spoken of the Lord (Heb. Yahveh) by the prophet, saying, (23) Behold, a virgin shall be with child, and shall bring forth a son, and they shall call his name Emmanuel, which being interpreted is, God with us." For this wonderful "prophecy" of the Virgin-birth of the Child Jesus, the marginal reference is to the Old Testament, Book of Isaiah, Chapter vii, v. 14, as the inspired "source" of the assertion made by Matthew. True, it says nothing of any miraculous pregnancy of any woman by the Holy Ghost, who was wholly unknown in the Old Testament; but this we do find, as rendered by the "false pen of the Scribes" who translated Isaiah:

"Therefore, the Lord himself shall give you a sign: behold, a virgin shall conceive, and bear a son, and shall call his name Immanuel" (Is. vii, 14).

The King James, or Authorized Version or Translation, puts into the margin opposite this verse, the words "Or, Thou, O Virgin, shalt call" etc. Nothing like this is in the Hebrew text. We turn to the Hebrew text of this most wonderful of the "prophecies"; and may well be amazed to find that it is falsely translated. The actual Hebrew words, read from right to left, and transliterated into English letters, so that the reader who knows not Hebrew may at least "catch" some words, the sacred words are: "laken yittan adonai hu lakem oth hinneh Tm-almah harah ve-yeldeth ben ve-karath shem-o immanuel."

Literally translated into English, in the exact order of the Hebrew words, the original "prophecy" truly reads: "Therefore shall-give my-lord he (himself) to you sign behold the- maid conceived (is pregnant) and-bear-eth son and.-call-eth name-his Immanuel."

Here the word "harah" (conceived) is the Hebrew Perfect tense, which as in English represents past and completed action; there is

not the remotest hint of future tense or time. No Doctor of Divinity or scholar in Hebrew can or will deny this. Moreover, this is confirmed by the more honest, yet deceptive Revised Version. In its text of Isaiah vii, 14, it copies word for word the false translation of the King James; but it inserts figures in the text after the words "a virgin" and "shall conceive," and puts into the margin opposite, in small type, which not one in many thousands ever read or would understand the significance of the true reading: "the virgin" and "is with child." It was thus not some indefinite "a virgin" 750 years in future, who in the future "shall conceive" and shall bear a son, and "shall call" his name Immanuel; but it was some present, known and designate maiden, to whom the "prophecy" referred, who had already conceived, or was already pregnant and with child; and whose offspring should be the "sign" which "my lord" would give to Ahaz. The honesty of the Translators and of Matthew in perverting this text of Isaiah into a "prophecy" of Jesus Christ is apparent.

THE "SIGN" OF A FALSE PROPHECY

What really was Isaiah "prophesying" about and whereof was the "sign" which he persisted in thrusting upon Ahaz after the King had flatly refused to listen to it and had piously protested that "I will not ask (for a sign), neither will I tempt Yahveh"?

No lawyer or other intelligent person would for a moment jump at the meaning of a document from an isolated paragraph; would stultify himself if he should pretend to form or render an opinion without a careful study of the whole document. The passage on which the opinion is sought must be taken with all its context or other contents of the document. Knowledge of the whole must therefore be had before the meaning of any pertinent passage can be understood.

As this of the "prophecy" of the alleged "Virgin-birth of Jesus Christ" is the key-stone of the arch of the whole scheme of Christianity, it is of the highest importance to know and clearly understand, from the context, what Isaiah is recorded as so oracularly delivering himself about. The whole of Chapter vii, or its material verses bearing upon the subject-matter of his "prophecy" must of necessity be presented to the reader.

In a word, Isaiah was speaking of a then pending war waged against Ahaz and Judah by the Kings of Israel and Syria, who we're besieging Jerusalem; Isaiah volunteered his "virgin-born sign" in proof of his "prophecy" shown false by the sequel that the siege and war would fail by the defeat of the allied Kings. Here is the inspired text with its full context:

"1. And it came to pass in the days of Ahaz, son of, etc., King of Judah, that Rezin the King of Syria, and Pekah the King of Israel, went up toward Jerusalem to war against it, but could not prevail against it. 3. Then said Yahveh unto Isaiah, go forth now to meet Ahaz, 4. and say unto him, take heed, and be quiet; fear not, neither be faint-hearted. 7. Thus saith Yahveh Elohim, it shall not stand, neither shall it come to pass. . .. "10. Moreover, Yahveh spoke again unto Ahaz (here Isaiah is not the medium), saying, 11. Ask a sign of Yahveh thy God; ask it either in the depth, or in the height above. 12. But Ahaz said, I will not ask, neither will I tempt Yahveh. 13. And he said, Hear ye now, O house of David; Is it a small thing for you to weary men, but will ye weary my God also? (here apparently Isaiah or some unknown medium is again speaking).

"14. Therefore, my Lord (Heb. Adonai, my lord) himself shall give you a sign; (honestly translated): behold, the maid is with child, and beareth a son and calleth his name Immanuel."

"15. Butter and honey, shall he eat, that he may know to refuse the evil, and choose the good. 16. For before the child shall know to refuse the evil, and choose the good, (that is, quite soon after its birth) the land that thou abhor shall be forsaken of both her kings."

This about eating butter and honey, so that the Child should know good from evil, is none too lucid of meaning; nor the assurance that before this should come about, "the land which thou abhor shall be forsaken of both her kings," is hardly more intelligible. But if meaning it has, it means as elucidated in Chapter viii that very soon after the promised "sign," Samaria, the land of Israel and its king Pekah, under the suzerainty of Rezin king of Syria, should be overthrown; and that the two kings should not prevail in their war against Judah.

The following vv. 17 to 24, to the end of Chapter vii, and which give the unique information that "Yahveh shall hiss for the fly that is in

Egypt and for the bee that is in the land of Assyria" (v. 18), and assure us that "Yahveh shall shave with a razor which is hired" (v. 20), are altogether too oracular and cabalistic for modern understanding; but their perusal is recommended as a rare bit of in- spiration.

Isaiah carries his peculiar line of "prophecy" over into Chapter viii, and after several verses utterly unintelligible, strikes the trail of his war prophecy again, thus: "5. Yahveh also spoke unto me again, saying, 6. Forasmuch as this people . . . rejoice in Rezin and in Remaliah's son (Pekah): 7. Now, therefore, behold, Yahveh bringeth upon them the King of Assyria, and all his glory; 8. And he shall pass through Judah; he shall overflow and go over; and the stretching out of his wings shall fill the breadth of thy land, O Immanuel."

No clearer proof could be that Isaiah, whatever he was trying to say, was not speaking of Jesus. In Chapter vii, he spoke of the war of the kings Rezin and Pekah, son of Remaliah, and offered a "sign" that their expedition would fail, this sign being the virgin born child Immanuel. Immediately afterwards he predicts a further war upon Judah by the King of Assyria, and addresses his allocation to this same unborn or infant Immanuel, and says that Assyria will overrun "thy land, O Immanuel." Isaiah spoke simply, and falsely, of a "sign" to King Ahaz, as to the then pending war. Yet Matthew says that this Immanuel was a prophecy of Jesus; but how Jesus could be Immanuel and a "sign" of the result of a war 750 years previously, or the subject of the remarks of Isaiah about the Assyrian war of the same period, is not explained in any revelation I have yet come across. This pretense by Matthew is clearly un- founded and false. Moreover, as this "sign" of the virgin-born child Immanuel, was proclaimed by Isaiah as a proof of the truth of his prophecy, I call special attention to the historical record of the result of this expedition of the Kings of Syria and Israel against Jerusalem and Ahaz.

This is from the second volume of the Chronicles of Israel and Judah, Chapter xxviii, as follows: "(1) Ahaz reigned sixteen years in Jerusalem: but he did not that which was right in the sight of Yahveh. (5) Wherefore Yahveh his God delivered him into the hand of the king of Syria; and they smote him, and carried away a great multitude of them captives, and brought them to Damascus. And he was also delivered into the hand of the king of Israel, who smote him with a great slaughter. (6) For Pekah the son of Remaliah slew in Judah a hundred and twenty thousand in one day, which were all valiant men: because they had forsaken Yahveh Elohim of their fathers. (8) And the children of Israel carried away captive of their brethren two hundred thousand women, sons, and daughters, and took also away much spoil from them, and brought them to Samaria."

So, the "prophecy" is seen of itself to be false.

THE "PROPHECIES" OF JESUS CHRIST

2. WHERE THE KING WAS BORN

The second statement made by Matthew, in which he appeals to the prophets, is in Chapter ii, vv. 1 to 6, that when the "Wise Men" came from the East to Jerusalem in search of the newborn "King of the Jews," Herod sent for the chief priests and scribes and "demanded of them where Christ should be born." How Herod could call a baby a few days old, of whom he knew nothing, "Christ," is beside the present issue. "Christ" means "anointed," and Jesus was not "anointed" in any sense until thirty-odd years later, the woman broke the box of ointment over him just before his death.

But Matthew asserts, in vv. 5 and 6: "And they said unto him, In Bethlehem of Judea; for thus is it written by the prophet, (6) And thou Bethlehem, in the land of Judah^ art not the least among the princes of Judah; for out of thee shall come a Governor, that shall rule my people Israel." The marginal source reference of this prophecy is the Book of Micah, Chapter v, v. 2. This, with its pertinent context, reads as follows:

"(2) But thou, Bethlehem Ephrathah, though thou be little among the thousands of Judah, yet out of thee shall he come forth unto me that is to be ruler in Israel; whose goings forth have been from of old, from everlasting. (5) And this man shall be the peace, "when the Assyrian shall come into our land: and when he shall tread in our palaces, then shall we raise against him seven shepherds and eight principal men. (6) And they shall waste the land of Assyria with the sword, and the land of Nimrod: thus, shall he deliver us from the Assyrian, when he cometh into our land, and when he treadeth within our borders." Now, whatever this may have referred to, it referred to some leader who should arise to oppose the Assyrians. Nineveh, "that great city," the capital of Assyria, was destroyed, and Assyrian power ceased to exist, 606 years before Christ. This makes it most evident that Micah had no reference to Jesus; and it may seem an oddity that the chief priests and scribes, who always opposed and denied Jesus during his life, and sent him to his death, should have wittingly furnished Matthew with so potent a prophecy concerning him, when Jesus was but a few days old. If the chief priests and scribes knew that the infant Jesus was the Messiah, the fulfillment of Micah's prophecy, some may wonder why they did not help him to become indeed "a ruler in Israel" and its great deliverer.

Is IT GOD'S WOBD?

3. "Out OF EGYPT"

Matthew's third invocation of the prophets, although the matter referred to was a past fact and not a prophecy of future fact, is also found in Chapter ii, when the Angel is said to have appeared to Joseph in a dream and told him to take Jesus to Egypt in order to escape Herod. I quote verses, where Joseph,

"(14) When he arose, he took the young child and his mother by night, and departed into Egypt: (15) And was there until the death of Herod: that it might be fulfilled which was spoken of Yahveh by the prophet, saying, Out of Egypt have I called my son." The marginal reference for the source of this prophecy is to Hosea (xi, 1). This chapter is entitled by the Bible editors, "The ingratitude of Israel unto God for his benefits," and refers entirely to the past record of the people of Israel. I quote v. 1, supplemented by v. 5, which read:

"(1) When Israel was a child, then I loved him, and called my son out of Egypt. . .. (5) He shall not return into the land of Egypt, but the Assyrian shall be his king, because they refused to return." Now, there is a marginal reference at this passage (v. 1), which refers to Exodus, iv, 2223, as the source of Hosea's allusion to the people called "Israel" as the "son" of Yahveh, and refers to the fact of this "son" being in Egypt, and being "called" out of Egypt by Moses. Never once does the text say "I will call" but "called."

The historical allusion, with its context, is as follows:

"(21) And Yahveh said unto Moses, (22) thou shalt say unto Pharaoh, Thus, saith Yahveh, Israel is my son, even my first born; (23) and I say unto thee, let my son go, that he may serve me."

From this it is clear that Hosea was looking into the far past and speaking of the exodus of the children of Israel out of Egypt; and was not peering into the dim future and speaking of the flight of the Joseph family into Egypt. So, Matthew makes another false appeal to "prophecy."

4. "OUT-HERODING" HEROD

The fourth venture of Matthew citing the prophets is in the same Chapter (ii, 1718), after relating the "Massacre of the Innocents

THE "PROPHECIES" OF JESUS CHRIST

cents" by Herod in his effort to murder the infant Jesus. I quote those verses, in which Matthew states:

"(17) Then was fulfilled that which was spoken by Jeremy the prophet, saying (13) In Rama there was a voice heard, lamentation, and weeping, and great mourning, Rachel weeping for her children, and would not be comforted, because they are not." The marginal reference opposite this citation is to the Book of Jeremiah (xxxi, 15). The weeping Prophet was speaking of the utter desolation of the people on account of the Babylonian captivity, and threats of further destruction by Nebuchadnezzar, as any one reading the Chapter may see. I quote the verse referred to, which is as follows:

"(15) Thus saith Yahveh: A voice was heard in Ramah, lamentation and bitter weeping; Rachel weeping for her children refused to be comforted for her children, because they were not."

Jeremiah speaks of an event already happened, and quotes Yahveh as speaking in the past tense "a voice was heard," because of the great afflictions caused by the Babylonians over 600 years before the episode related of Herod. The reader may draw his own conclusions as to the honesty of Matthew's use of this "prophecy" and its fulfillment under Herod. And not a word of uninspired human history records such an impossible massacre by the Roman King.

5. THE "NAZARENE"

The fifth in order occurs in the same Chapter (ii, 23), referring to their residence upon the return of Joseph and Jesus from Egypt. I quote it as follows:

"(23) And he came and dwelt in a city called Nazareth: that it might be fulfilled which was spoken by the prophets, He shall be called a Nazarene."

This is a bit of fancy falsehood. There is not a word of mention in the Old Testament of such a place as Nazareth nor of Nazarenes.

The marginal references to this v. 23 are two, Judges xiii, 5, and 1 Samuel, i, 11. These verses, and their context, refer to matters so far removed from Matthew's alleged "prophecy," that it is idle to quote them. But here they are. In the first instance, the of Manoah was childless; an Angel of Yahveh appeared to her, and said: "(5) Lo, thou shalt conceive, and bear a son; and no razor shall come on his head: for the child shall be a Nazarite (Heb. Nazir) unto God from the womb: and he shall begin to deliver Israel out of the hand of the Philistines/'

The product of this angelic visitation was the giant-killer Samson, and he was to fight the Philistines; Jesus never did. The second reference has to do with a like angelic aid to Hannah, who made a vow to never let a razor come upon the head of her prospective son Samuel. Those unkempt offspring of angelic intercourse were called Nazarites. This is the closest that the Old Testament gets to Nazareth, and its inhabitant Nazarenes. So, Matthew's invocation of the "prophets" is far afield both in form and substance.

6. THE GREAT LIGHT

The sixth so-called "prophecy" relating to Jesus, which Matthew invokes in this behalf, is in Chapter iv, 1216, a paragraph standing unrelated to anything else in the Chapter. I copy the verses as follows:

"(12) Now when Jesus had heard that John was cast into prison, he departed into Galilee; (13) And leaving Nazareth, he came and dwelt in Capernaum, which is upon the sea coast, in the borders of Zebulon and Naphthalin: (14) That it might be fulfilled which was spoken by Esaias the prophet, saying, (15) The land of Zebulon, and the land of Naphthalin, by the way of the sea, beyond Jordan, Galilee of the Gentiles; (16) The people which sat in darkness saw a great light; and to them which sat in the region and shadow of death light is sprung up."

We are given as marginal reference of authority for this, Isaiah ix, 12. As Matthew so mutilates and distorts his quotation, I shall have to direct attention of the reader to the several marked discrepancies and contortions which he makes of his texts, and explain, by their context, what Isaiah was really saying:

"(1) Nevertheless the dimness shall not be such as was in her vexation, when at the first he lightly afflicted the land of Zebulun, and the land of Naphtali, and afterwards did more grievously afflict her by the way of the sea, beyond Jordan, in Galilee of the nations. (2) The people that walked in darkness have seen a great light: they that dwell in the land of the shadow of death, upon them hath the light shined."

THE "PROPHECIES" OF JESUS CHRIST

It will be noticed that Matthew entirely omits all the words which show that Isaiah was speaking of some past and accomplished historical fact, relating to the afflictions which the tribal sections mentioned had already suffered. These explanatory and historical words, to repeat them for the reader's better catching their significance, are: "Nevertheless, the dimness shall not be such as (was) in her vexation, when at the first he lightly afflicted Zebulon and Naphthali, and afterwards did more grievously afflict her." After thus, depriving the verse of all sense, Matthew retains the simple geographical names as follows: "the land of Zabulon, and the land of Nephthalim, by the way of the sea, beyond Jordan, Galilee of the Gentiles." And he converts these meaningless words, taken out of their sense in a historical past context, into a prophecy, which he says was fulfilled because Jesus went to the town of Capernaum in that part of the country.

But there is more to it, to which I will briefly call attention, for better understanding. The verse opens with the words "nevertheless the dimness." Necessarily this refers to something which has preceded in the text. This is found in Chapter viii, of which Chapter ix is simply a continuation. But Chapter viii is so incoherent, speaking of "seeking unto them that have familiar spirits, and unto wizards that peep, and that mutter," that it is hardly possible to know what Isaiah is "raving" about. However, in the last v. 22, he denounces such seekers after wizards, and delivers himself of this: "(22) And they shall look unto the earth; and behold trouble and darkness, dimness of anguish; and they shall be driven to darkness." Then Chapter ix opens with the words quoted, "Nevertheless, the dimness shall not be such as was in her vexation, when at the first he lightly afflicted the land of Zebulun and the land of Naphthali, and afterwards did more grievously afflict her," etc. Isaiah then continues, in v. 2: "The people that walked in darkness have seen a great light," etc. All this, whatever unapparent sense there may be in it, refers to past facts and events, and the reader may judge of Matthew's accuracy in calling it a "prophecy" fulfilled by Jesus going to Capernaum.

7. HE BORE OUR INFIRMITIES

The seventh appeal of Matthew to "prophecy" is in Chapter viii, 16-17, which are as follows:

"(16) When the even was come, they brought unto him many that were possessed with devils: and he cast out the spirits with his word, and healed all that were sick; (17) That it might be fulfilled which was spoken by Esaias the prophet, saying, Himself took our infirmities, and bare our sicknesses." For this the marginal reference carries us to Isaiah liii, 4, which I copy as follows:

"Surely, he hath borne our griefs, and carried our sorrows: yet we did esteem him stricken, smitten of God, and afflicted."

All this is in the past tense, showing Isaiah lamenting over some "departed friend," who was esteemed to have been "smitten of God," and now dead. It can have no possible reference to Jesus Christ, Yahveh's "beloved son in whom I am well pleased," engaged in the divine work of casting out devils and healing the sick and smitten; never was Jesus at any time "smitten of God." So, Matthew again uses a few words out of their context, misquotes them at that, and calls a lamenting statement over some past fact a "prophecy" of future event.

8. THE "BRUISED REED"

The eighth instance of Matthew in adapting what he calls "prophecy" to his own uses, as proof that his account is the truth, occurs in Chapter xii, vv. 14* to 21. The passage is long, but as it is necessary to compare it with the reputed "prophecy" in order to show Matthew's singular misquotation, and misuse, I copy it entire as follows:

"(14) Then the Pharisees went out, and held a council against him, how they might destroy him. (15) But when Jesus knew it, he withdrew himself from thence: and great multitudes followed him, and he healed them all; (16) And charged them that they should not make him known;

(17) That it might be fulfilled which was spoken by Esaias the prophet, saying, (18) Behold my servant, whom I have chosen; my beloved in whom my soul is well pleased: I will put my spirit upon him, and he shall shew judgment to the Gentiles. (19) He shall not strive, nor cry; neither shall any man hear his voice in the streets. (20) A bruised reed shall he not break, and smoking flax shall he not quench, till he sends forth judgment unto victory. (21) And in his name shall the Gentiles trust." The marginal reference for the source of this is Isaiah, xlii, 1-4, as follows:

"(1) Behold my servant, whom I uphold; mine elect, in whom my soul delighted; I have put my spirit upon him: he shall bring forth judgment to the Gentiles. (2) He shall not cry, nor lift up, nor cause his voice to be heard in the street. (3) A bruised reed shall he not break, and the smoking flax shall he not quench: he shall bring forth judgment unto truth. (4) He shall not fail nor be discouraged, till he has set judgment in the earth: and the isles shall wait for his law."

Who "my servant" upon whom "I have" put my spirit, here? spoken of is, Isaiah does not tell us; but certainly, the description does not in the least fit Jesus. Jesus was discouraged, and he enjoined secrecy on all his followers and fled to Gethsemane, where he collapsed in despair, as the whole unhappy scene in the Garden shows, and he never saw "victory"! And Isaiah never at all said what Matthew attributes to him in v. 21:

"And in his name shall the Gentiles trust"; this is entirely new, made of the whole cloth, and the whole "prophecy" is misquoted and misapplied.

9. "THE KING COMETH"

The ninth resort by Matthew to this method of proof that things done by Jesus were fulfillment of ancient prophecy, is found in Chapter xxi, vv. 1 to 5, which are as follows:

"(1) And when they drew nigh into Jerusalem, and were come to Bethphage, unto the mount of Olives, then sent Jesus two disciples, (2) Saying unto them, Go into the village over against you, and straightway ye shall find an ass tied, and a colt with her: loose them, and bring them unto me. (3) And if any man say ought unto you, ye shall say, The Lord hath need of them; and straightway he will send them. (4) All this was done, that it might be fulfilled which was spoken by the prophet, saying, (5) Tell ye the daughter of Sion, Behold, thy king cometh unto thee, meek, and sitting upon an ass, and a colt the foal of an ass."

This is an "ass" misquotation of alleged prophecy, as is shown by turning to the marginal reference, Zechariah, ix, 9, which I quote as follows:

"(9) Rejoice greatly, O daughter of Zion; shout, O daughter of Jerusalem: behold, thy King cometh unto thee: he is just, and having salvation; lowly, and riding upon an ass, and upon a colt the foal of an ass. "The Book of Zechariah treats of the return of parts of the Jewish tribes from captivity in Babylon, by leave of King Darius; and Zechariah is very jubilant over it, and indulges in some very flighty exultations about it. In the previous Chapter viii, Zechariah declares:

(8) "Thus, saith Yahveh of hosts: behold, I will save my people from the east country, and from the west country; (9) And I will bring them, and they shall dwell in the midst of Jerusalem." And, in Chapter ix, after the "ass entry of the King," and amid other exultations, Zechariah exclaims, in further evidence that he was speaking of the "return from captivity," and not of Jesus entering Jerusalem:

"(12) Turn you to the strong hold, ye prisoners of hope: (16) And Yahveh their God shall save them in that day: (17) For how great is his goodness, and how great is his beauty! corn shall make the young men cheerful, and new wine the maids.

5'

Zechariah is not here very lucid, but in any event, he was exulting over the "return of the captivity," and not over Jesus Christ, as Matthew would have believed.

10. WHAT is THIS ONE?

Matthew's tenth appeal to the prophets, Chapter xxvi, 51-56, is too general to permit of specific contradiction by comparing his authority. I refer to those verses, but will simply state their substance. It is the story of Peter cutting off the ear of the high priest's servant with a sword, on the night of the arrest of Jesus. Jesus told him to put up his sword, and said that he could call down twelve legions of angels to his defense if he should pray for them. And he asks:

"(54) But then how shall the scriptures be fulfilled, that thus it must be?" Then Matthew puts in, and says:

"(56) But all this was done, that the scriptures of the prophets might be fulfilled." He does not say which scriptures nor which prophets; but the Bible editors come to his aid and give a marginal reference to the much abused Isaiah (liii, 7), which we have above referred to and shown to be all in the past tense, in which Isaiah bewails his anonymous "departed friend" who was "smitten of God." Another editorial reference is far afield to the Book of Lamentations, iv, 20, which may be offered for what it is worth:

"(20) The breath of our nostrils, the anointed of Yahveh, was taken in their pits, of whom he said, under his shadow shall we live among the heathen," The Lamentator is here bewailing the desolation of Jerusalem under the captivity of the "heathen" Babylonians, as appears from the entire epic of woe, but particularly in the preceding verses 11 and 12, which I quote in this connection.

"(11) Yahveh hath accomplished his fury; he hath poured out his fierce anger, and hath kindled a fire in Zion, and it hath devoured the foundations thereof. (12) The kings of the earth, and all the inhabitants of the world, would not have believed that the adversary and the enemy should have entered into the gates of Jerusalem."

So, it is plain that the writer was speaking of the ruin of Jerusalem. But it further appears of whom he was speaking by the terms "the breath of our nostrils, the anointed of Yahveh." All the Jewish Kings were the "anointed of Yahveh" just as modern ones also are said to be. A marginal reference opposite these words of Lamentations is to Jeremiah, lii, 9, which I will quote together with the preceding verse 8, so as to get the full context.

"(8) But the army of the Chaldeans pursued after the king, and over- took Zedekiah in the plains of Jericho; and all his army was scattered from him. (9) Then they took the king, and carried him up unto the king of Babylon to Riblah in the land of Hamath, where he gave judgment upon him." And for full measure of the woe which moved the Lamentations, I add verse 10:

"And the king of Babylon slew the sons of Zedekiah before his eyes: he slew also all the princes of Judah in Riblah." Hinc ttlae lacrimae! So, Matthew is seen again twisting historical past facts into pretended prophecies fulfilled by Jesus.

11. THE "POTTER'S FIELD"

For the eleventh time Matthew tells us something, and invokes the prophets, the passage being the story of Judas and the thirty pieces of silver, in Chapter xxvii, 3-10, which I refer to, and state the substance. Matthew says that Judas repented of his bargain of betrayal and took the money back to the chief priests; and threw the money at their feet and went and hanged himself. The holy priests who had paid the thirty pieces for the "betrayal of innocent blood," were punctilious about putting the price of the blood back into the treasury of Yahveh, so

"(7) They took counsel, and bought with them the potter's field, to bury strangers in. (8) Wherefore that field is called, The field of blood, unto this day.

(9) Then was fulfilled that which was spoken by Jeremy the prophet, saying, and they took the thirty pieces of silver, the price of him that was valued, whom they of the children of Israel did value; (10) And gave them for the potter's field, as Yahveh appointed me."

If I were arguing this as a case in court, I would indict this in strong terms. But as I am simply offering appeals to "prophecy" with a little necessary comment, I merely let the reader compare it with Jeremiah's words, in his Chapter xxxii, 6-15, to which I refer the reader. But as they have no more to do with the high priests' buying the potter's field with the thirty pieces of silver, then they have to do with my buying my house in this City, I will not copy them into the record. They simply refer to Hanameel coming to Jeremiah in prison, "according to the word of Yahveh," and saying to him,

"(8) Buy my field, I pray thee, that is in Anathoth; (9) And I bought the field of Hanameel, my uncle's son, that was in Anathoth and weighed him the money, even seventeen shekels of silver."

- v This is all there is to "that which was spoken by Jeremy the prophet," pretended to be fulfilled by buying the potter's field with the blood money of Judas Iscariot.

But the Bible editors give another marginal reference, not to "Jeremy the prophet," but to Zechariah, Chapter xi, 10-14, for the reason, presumably, that a "potter" and "thirty pieces of silver" are mentioned. So that no opportunity to let Matthew and his editors vindicate themselves even once may be denied them, I quote these incoherent verses, without comment, as they are not worth it only to say, what the reader can readily see, that they have no earthly connection with Iscariot's thirty pieces, or with anything else sanely imaginable:

"(10) And I took my staff, even Beauty, and cut it asunder, that I might break my covenant which I had made with all the people. (11) And it was broken in that day: and so, the poor of the flock that waited upon me knew that it was the word of Yahveh. (12) And I said unto them, if ye think good, give me my price; and if not, forbear. So, they weighed for my price thirty pieces of silver. (13) And Yahveh said unto me, cast it unto the potter; a good price that I was prized at of them. And I took the thirty pieces of silver, and cast them to the potter in the house of Yahveh. (14) Then I cut asunder mine other staff, even Bands, that I might break the brotherhood between Judah and Israel."

JUDAS HANGED HIMSELF?

Before passing from Matthew's story of Judas, who, he says, (verse 5) "departed, and went, and hanged himself," I may call attention to the fact that Matthew is flatly contradicted on this point by whoever wrote "The Acts of the Apostles" (supposed to be the Evangelist Luke). This authority, also indulging in some dubious references, makes Peter tell a different story from Matthew, as appears from Chapter i, 15-18, as follows:

"(15) And in these days Peter stood up in the midst of the disciples, and said, (16) Men and brethren, this scripture must needs have been fulfilled, which the Holy Ghost by the mouth of David spoke before concerning Judas, which was guide to them that took Jesus. (17) For he was numbered with us and had obtained part of this ministry. (18)

Now this man purchased a field with the reward of iniquity; and falling headlong he burst asunder in the midst and all his bowels gushed out." As is seen, according to this delicate gloat over the fate of an apostate brother apostle, it was Iscariot himself that bought a field and not a "potter's field" but an estate with the thirty pieces which he had received as "the reward of iniquity"; he did not, therefore, "repent" and return the money to the priests, and go hang himself; but he accidentally fell and ruptured himself fatally.

Peter's reference to David as speaking, one thousand years previously, of Judas, is of a piece with some of the false pretenses of Peter's pretended "successors" ever since. The side reference for David's reputed remarks about Judas, is to Psalms xli, 9, which I quote: "Yea, mine own familiar friend, in whom I trusted, which did eat of my bread, hath lifted up his heel against me."

Now, David had troubles of his own, without bothering himself with Judas a thousand years ahead. The whole Psalm xli shows that Peter ignorantly or willfully falsified. David was pleading with Yahveh for himself alone, as appears by the verses which I will quote:

"(4) I said, Yahveh, he merciful unto me: heal my soul; for I have sinned against thee. (5) Mine enemies speak evil of me, when shall he die, and his name perish? . . . (9) Yea, mine own familiar friend, in whom I trusted, which did eat of my bread, hath lifted up his heel against me. (10) But thou, Yahveh, be merciful unto me, and raise me up, that I may require them."

No words are needed to show that David was speaking of his own present troubles, and nothing else. And he prays his Yahveh to be merciful and raise him up, so that he could take vengeance on his enemy. And David says no such thing as "he was numbered among us, and had obtained part of this ministry." This is a pure invention of Peter, often imitated by his "Successors" since. In this connection, read Acts i, v. 19, about the "field of blood," which flatly contradicts Matt, xxvii, 78, as to the origin of the term; and the finish of Peter's false appeals to "prophecy" by David regarding Judas, "and his bishopric let another take" (Acts i, 20), is shown absolutely false and ridiculous by the reference cited, (Ps. cix, 8), as the context of the whole Psalm makes clear as day.

12. PARTING His GARMENTS

The twelfth and last of Matthew's appeals to the prophets which we will here notice is indulged at the time of all others when the occasion would seem to have led him to quote accurately and to tell the truth. In Chapter xxvii, 35, right under the shadow of the Cross, he says:

"(35) And they crucified him, and parted his garments, casting lots; that it might be fulfilled which was spoken by the prophet, they parted my garments among them, and upon my vesture did they cast lots." The reference is to Psalm xxii, 18, where David is again made responsible for a pretended prophecy though David is not usually, like Saul, "numbered among the prophets." Matthew misquotes the words of David, spoken in the present tense, and puts them into the past tense, and changes the pronoun "my" to "him," to make it apply to the acts of the Roman soldiers. I quote the words of David:

"(18) They part my garments among them, and cast lots upon me vesture." Again, David is bewailing his own troubles, in the fanciful imagery of Oriental poetry. He begins the Psalm, which is a song inscribed "to the Chief Musician Aijeleth," with the same words quoted by Jesus on the Cross: "My God, my God, why hast thou forsaken me!" and proceeds in language which he himself calls "the words of my roaring." Among the many "roaring" things he says about himself, I quote a very few:

"(12) Many bulls have compassed me; (13) They gaped upon me with their mouths, as a ravening and roaring lion. (14) All my bones are out of joint: my heart is like wax; it is melted in the midst of my bowels (David evidently wasn't up on anatomy, and didn't know of the diaphragm). (16) For dogs have compassed me: the assembly of the wicked have enclosed me: they pierced my hands and my feet (Wonder that Matthew didn't use this apt phrase as a prophecy of what they did to Jesus!) (17) I may tell all my bones: they look and stare upon me."

Then follows the casting of lots over his clothes. How far these "words of roaring" applied to Jesus on the Cross, as Matthew avers one verse of them did, and how correct Matthew is in his use of so-called prophecy, I leave now with the reader, for this is the end of Matthew's dealings with the Prophets. I pass now to Mark. /Is It Gods Word

Now if all of these so-called prophecies are not about Jesus, then what does this tell us? The religion is not true, period! What about his second coming that every one is waiting on? Let's take a quick look at this also: The crowning disproof of the Divinity, even of the common sense of truth of the Christ, and a sad proof of the serious delusion which he suffered, is the stupendous assertion which he made of his immediate second coming to earth in all the glory of his triumphant Kingdom. A more positive and explicit thing incapable of misunderstanding or double meaning he never said than this:

"Verily I say unto you, there be some standing here, which shall not taste of death, till they see the Son of Man (Ben-Adam) coming in his Kingdom" (Matt, xvi, 28; Mark, ix, 1).

"Verily I say unto you, that this generation shall not pass, till all these things be done" (Mark xiii, 30).

"But I tell you of a truth, that there be some standing here, which shall not taste of death, till they see the Kingdom of God" (Luke ix, 27).

And Caiaphas, the High Priest, before whom Jesus was led after his capture in the Garden, solemnly appealed to him for truth:

"I adjure thee by the Living God, that thou tell us whether thou be the Christ, the Son of God."

"Jesus saith unto him, thou hast said: nevertheless, I say unto you, Hereafter shall ye see the Son of Man sitting on the right hand of power, and coming in the clouds of heaven" (Matt, xxvi, 63-64; Mark xiv, 61-62).

And in these Nineteen Hundred years this supreme avowal of the Son of Yahveh has gone unverified. No more is needed to convict the inspired records of utter fallacy and discredit; to prove to demonstration that the lowly Nazarene was no God, was no Promised Messiah, but was himself a "false Christ," who has deceived the Very Elect of those who have had a misplaced Faith in his Holy Word.

CHAPTER 2

    Let's go back to the old testament for a while, shall we? What do we find here? We will find the same shit that we found in the new, this I promise, for this is where the new was to be taken from. Intolerance is the name I give to all religions for the most part. It doesn't matter what form it takes or what it believes in, for all religions on this planet are basically the same. The christians showed no mercy to those whom they perceived to be heretics or outright evil people, they had no tolerance for anyone who defied them or the powers of their day. So why should the priests of the Judaic religion be any different.

    The holy god of Israel who is also called merciful decreed on the mount of Sinai that:

    He that sacrifices to any gods {Elohim} save unto the Lord God [YHVH, Yahweh, Jehovah] alone, he shall be utterly destroyed. /Ex 22:20

    Plus, we have this being said by this most loving merciful god:

    If they brother, the son of thy mother, or thy son or thy daughter, or the wife of thy bosom, or thy friend, which is as thy own soul, entice thee saying, let us go serve other gods, thou shall not consent unto him, nor hearken unto him, neither shall thy eye pity him, neither shall thou spare neither shalt thou conceal him, BUT THOU SHALT SURELY KILL HIM;THY HAND SHALL BE THE FIRST UPON HIM TO DEATH, AND AFTERWARDS THE HAND OF ALL THE PEOPLE, AND THOU SHALT STONE HIM WITH STONES, THAT HE DIE!/Duet 13:6-9

This is the word of the god called merciful! This is the god called loving and this is the god that all depend on for their salvation! Does this sound like a god we would want to follow???? But even the priests much like the disciples of Jesus hold a lot of power, for here in the old just as in the new we find decrees like this:

The man that will do presumptuously, and will not hearken unto the priest, even this man shall die! /Deut 17:12

Why am I going through all of this to show that the Bible in both old and new testaments are not to be trusted? Because of one fact that is told in the old testament:

Wherefore I gave them also statutes that were not good, and judgments whereby they should not live. And I polluted them in their own gifts, in that they caused to pass through the fire all that openeth the womb, that I might make them desolate, to the end that they might know that I am the Lord. /Ez 20:25-26

The supposed god called merciful and loving, purposely gave Israel statutes that they could not live by, in other words he purposely gave them rules and laws they could never fulfill and, in this way, he could punish them at will. He then says he purposely polluted the sacrifices which in his own words were gifts from the womb, child sacrifice, for to go through the fire means to be sacrificed to Moloch. Listen to this:

The Angel Michael said, "yet there are still a few things we may do to secure our hold upon this world. We may find one feeble, before the poison takes stronger root, and impart unto him laws and rules to give unto the people.",

God told Michael," We cannot foster faith through the dictates of law."

Michael responded, "It is true, not through laws which dictate faith shall faith be derived. But rather, we shall dictate laws to which man, by his very nature, cannot adhere."

Michael continued," We shall give the divine law unto man that he cannot obey, then when he finds himself in disobedience he shall look to the heavens for grace and penance."

First came the law of provision so that the races of man would worship no other than the angelica, then came the laws of the beast, which forbid the cravings of that which is less evolved in man. Then came the laws of the mind, which made the thought just as bad as the deed.

In this way the angelica covered all of what man is and could be, the laws covered mind body instinct as well as spirit. The reason for this is because of one thing, our life with its stress and problems, its hurts and its up and downs all do one thing for these angelica.... sustain them! They feed off of us, and love it when we cry or are depressed, yet they love it when we pray to them in utmost joy as well, for both keep them fed very well.

Now you may say hey! Where did these verses come from, for I never read them in the bible, yes, your right, these come from a set of scriptures known as the Devils Apocrypha. A set of scriptures that explain so much of the bible and why god or the one in three as the DA {Devils Apocrypha} calls him, does what he does.

All it took for me was to read those verses above for me to get to where I am today. How does a god who says he is merciful, loving, take people called his children, or even his wife as Israel is sometimes called, and make the laws to where they cannot uphold them! No parent in their right mind would do this to their own children, and do this for the reason of letting them know who the parent is! That's horrible and parents like that would be arrested and jailed. Yet this god is looked at as being holy and great so that everyone praises him as such, and he is let off with all of the crimes he has committed.

CHAPTER 3

Then the day came when the angelica ripped a hole in the dimensions and they walked through and, they were here. They saw the life on this planet, and the one in 3 said this, "Only by the power of sentient faith may we survive here." Then when questioned by Raphael, for this angel feared man becoming more then human one day which would rival their power, god said this, "It need not be so, for with the powers of science may we manipulate the path of their lives."

So, this god which is nothing more than the toughest angel on the block, yet still only and angel tells us straight, manipulation! We have been manipulated ever since. We have had the wool pulled over our eyes and have been used to keep those above alive, while watching our own die!

The name Luicfer has been abused in so many ways because of the lies we have been told about him. What does this angel who is looked upon by most of us have to say about this plan of god? This is what the bringer of evil(supposed) has to say on this, "This is an evil thing thou would have us do! If it is our destiny to pass from this existence, then so be it! We have not the right to enslave others! Nor is it our right to shape their destiny for this universe is not our own!"

So, the one blamed for bringing all of the evil into the world is the very one wanting us to be our own masters, he protected us! Now this Lucifer also wanted to know something very simple, if all the angelica wished to do to us is so good and alright, then why does this universe not sustain them naturally, why do they have to manipulate others and feed off of their energy! This is the response given to Lucifer, "What natural law do we violate by raising sheep so that we may sustain ourselves?" so says the Almighty.

This is where the split or the war in heaven originated! The so-called demons were the ones protecting us, they were the ones who wanted us to grow naturally, and to be left alone! They didn't want a hand in making us to be cattle for the angelica, so they were cast out. Here is the punishment handed down to the followers of Lucifer as well as the Light Bearer Himself, the Almighty stated this, "Thy names shall be spoken as the names of treason, no longer shall ye be of us, and from the heaves shall ye be banished for all times. And thee Lucifer, the perpetrator of all of this vileness, thou shalt henceforth be known as Satan, the adversary, and those aligned with thee, shall be cursed among the righteous, and they shall be called demons, the corrupted ones, and thy Cherubim and Seraphim shall be known as Legion for many are their folly!" Now with this being said, let me also point this out, the pentagram inverted is the symbol of all of those who fought for us, yet it is seen as evil. This very star is the symbol of the fallen for one reason only for the stone which carried all of the fallen to earth was seen hitting the earth as a falling star, so that star pointing downward is in the earth, a circle, so we have the inverted star within the circle, the pentagram.

God then always kept a close watch on the creatures known as man, and when he so chose, he would alter the structure of our destiny, and from this type of manipulation arose new and better Creatures, so this is a way of saying, he altered our DNA, and in doing this he got different versions of us. The DA goes on to describe all of the experiments carried out on us and our DNA, so that this is where the different classifications of early man has come from. This was done until Homo Sapiens appeared through the DNA changes, for this was the species god was ready to work with for our manipulation was now to begin in earnest.

One thing the angelica found to be true is the fact that if they have to force us to give them our faith, they lose the very thing they seek to gain from us. Free will was the one thing they realized that man must have, yet they devised other ways to get to us and still give us free will.

They used what they called psychology and they used it with the part of early man's mind which was the most bestial, and they called it .... fear!

So, god appeared to the Adamic tribe, seeing there were others on this earth, and god told Adam to follow a star to a place where he and his tribe would be safe and protected by god, and it happened. So, Adam slowly began to call upon and praise this god, and it was a sweet savor unto god!

So, Adam was led to a garden oasis known as Eden, and Adam as well as his tribe gained favor in the eyes of god and the rest of the angelica. In this way did the angelica guide the tribe of Adam as well as other tribes in time.

As this was going on, Satan and the fallen ones were disgusted at what was transpiring on this earth, this is what was said by Satan himself, "only we wield the power to stop this atrocity. Should we fail in this our task, eternal torment shall befall mankind, for their lives shall hold only death, and in death they shall have no life."

Has this not been the case? We exist, we do not live! We are alive with no life, for we are the walking dead! We have no actual life in us, for we are nothing but a food source for these beings and we have remained in that fear so that mankind as a whole will never join with Satan and his host so we may fight for our freedom!

Now in the bible we see god warning Adam about eating of the fruit of the tree of knowledge, but there is no mention about the tree of life, why? The DA shows us that both trees were planted by the fallen, not by god as he would have us to think, the fallen gave us both trees, one for a long life and one for the knowledge we would need.

This is why god mentions nothing about the tree of life until after the tree of knowledge has been tasted, for god couldn't have us living long after having been given knowledge, could he?

Now if we return to the bible, we see in the supposed fall of man that god is the one who actually tells the first lie. For god told Adam that in the day he eats of the tree of knowledge, he shalt surely die, and this is what Eve told the serpent also. Yet the serpent told Eve this wasn't true, that their eyes would be open and they would be as gods knowing good and evil, he told Eve that god knew this. So, what does go do? He repeats the serpent verbatim, he says to those in heaven that the man has become one of us (one of the gods) knowing good and evil, and now if he eats of the tree of life and live forever. This he won't allow. Now I find it funny, god has no problem telling us that the prophets are lying in his name, nor does he have a problem telling us the scribes have changed his words, yet never does he tell the serpent that he lied, or because of his lying to Eve... all he says to the serpent is, "Because thou hast done thither art cursed...and so on. Not once did he accuse him of lying, he just seemed pissed the serpent told us what was going on, he told us the truth. Now did Adam and or Eve die? No!!!! Just as the serpent had said. Adam went on to live another 930 years. Now christians will tell you he died spiritually, but that does not fit in with the threat given to Adam.

So, what are we to do with all of this so far? Look at it with reason, with true intellect. We were lied to!

Now speaking of lies, as I said above, god has no problem telling us about humans lying, especially through the prophet Jeremiah, yet in Jeremiah 4:10 we hear the prophet proclaiming, Sovereign LORD, how completely you have deceived this people, and Jerusalem, by saying you will have peace, when the sword is at our throats."

This god even says this," My people are fools, they do not know me, they are senseless children, they have no understanding, they are skilled in doing evil they know not how to do good."

Can you believe what you have just read? He claims these children have no fucking clue who he is and have no clue how to do good, only evil. Yet why is this? Let me refresh your memory.

Wherefore I gave them also statutes that were not good, and judgments whereby they should not live. And I polluted them in their own gifts, in that they caused to pass through the fire all that opened the womb, that I might make them desolate, to the end that they might know that I am the Lord. /Ez 20:25-26

Now if god complains we only know evil and how to commit evil, should this not fall upon his shoulders? Seeing he has given us the "bad statutes, and polluted the gifts so causing child sacrifice" If he gave us all of this, is it not on him? Plus, there is this,

"I form the light and create darkness, I bring prosperity and create disaster, I the LORD do all these things. /Is45:7

Now in the King James Version we see instead of disasters we have the words "I make peace, and create evil"

We are nowhere done yet, for in Ecclesiastes we read, "Consider the work of the true god, for who can straighten out what he has made crooked?

On a good day reflect this goodness, but on the day of adversity, consider that god made the one as well as the other, so that men cannot be certain of anything in the future. /Eccl 7:13-14

Read this!!!! Did you read the above quotes? Why would god who is supposed to be so holy and righteous need to make anything crooked? Why would he give men good days as well as days of adversity so they could never be certain of anything now or in the future? Who fucking cruel!

Let's now look at this verse.

When a trumpet sounds in a city, do not the people tremble? When a disaster comes to a city, has not the LORD caused it? /Amos 3:6

Wow! It is the Lord who causes the disasters, brings evil, makes rich, makes poor, and he will mix it up so no one may be certain about their lives or those of their loved ones. Yet we are the children with no understanding, who only know evil! What a crock of shit! Yet has this god not said also:

"My people are fools; they do not know me.

If this isn't one of the truest of all statements in the whole of the bible, for how many truly know god?

CHAPTER 4

Now there is a set of scriptures in this day and age known as the Urantia Book. This is a collection of papers supposedly given by angelical beings or messengers to this planet which is known as Urantia. It's an interesting read if you have the time to invest for its well over 1000 pages. What I find so interesting though is this, this book describes the Lucifer rebellion in almost the same since as the Devils Apocrypha. How can this be? Could there be some truth to this book as well? Let's look at this section known as paper 53. Now mystically speaking, I find it no coincidence that it is paper 53, for in Isaiah chapter 53 we see the messiah spoken of, he who bore our pains and we cared not for him, for we thought him to be cursed and stricken from god. Is this not how Lucifer is perceived, could he be our Messiah?

The Urantia Book says this about the beginning of the Lucifer rebellion, Lucifer became a bold and earnest advocate for "self-assertion and liberty. "Let me repeat this,

Lucifer became a bold and earnest advocate for "self-assertion and liberty."

Now before we go on, let me explain a little more about the Urantia Book. It is full of beings with different titles and functions. It speaks of different Universes, or what I think are actually different dimensions. Yes, it speaks of god as well as God the Supreme, in fact whole sections are dedicated to this Supreme God who turns out to be a being who is still evolving into this Supreme god. So, our god is nothing more than a being who has lived for numerous millennia and has continued to evolve, while being served by numerous and different types of angels from multi different universes! It can be very confusing.

So, the rebellion manifested because this Lucifer wanted to assert or proclaim his own rights as well as liberty, or to be free! This is so fucked up huh? To want to have rights and be free, how could any of us stand with a being desiring that? Yes, I am being sarcastic. Let's look at his manifesto.

The Lucifer manifesto had three major points of contention, the first being,

1. The reality of the Universal Father:

Lucifer charged that the Universal Father did not really exist, that physical gravity and space energy were inherent in the universe and that the Father was a myth invented by the paradise sons (angelica) to enable them to maintain the rule of the universe in the Fathers name. He denied that personality was a gift of the universal Father. He even intimated, that the fin alters were in collusion with the paradise sons to foist fraud upon all of creation, since they never brought back a very clear-cut idea of the Fathers actual personality as it is discernable on paradise. He traded on reverence as ignorance,

2. The universe government of the creator son-Michael:

Lucifer contended that the local systems should be autonomous. He protested against the right of Michael the creator son, to assume sovereignty of Nebadan in the name of a hypothetical paradise father, and require all personalities to acknowledge allegiance to this unseen father. He asserted that the whole plan of worship was a clever scheme to aggrandize the paradise sons. He was willing to acknowledge Michael as his creator-father, but not as his god and rightful ruler.

Most bitterly did he attack the right of the Ancient of Days {Foreign Potentates} to interfere in the affairs of the local systems and universes, these rulers he denounced as tyrants and usurpers. He exhorted his followers to believe that none of these rulers could do ought to interfere with the operation of complete home rule if men as well as angels only had the courage to assert themselves and boldly claim their rights.

He contended that the executioners of the ancient of days could be debarred from functioning in the local systems if the native beings would only assert their independence, He maintained that immortality was inherent in the system personalities, that resurrection was natural and automatic, and that all beings would live eternally except for the arbitrary and unjust acts of the executioners of the ancient of days.

3. The attack on the plan of ascendant mortal training:

Lucifer maintained that far too much time and energy were expended upon the scheme of so thoroughly training ascending mortals in principles of universe administration, principles which he alleged were unethical, and unsound. He protests against the age long program for preparing the mortals of space for some unknown destiny, and pointed to the presence of the finalizer corps on Jerusem, as proof that these mortals had spent ages of preparation for some destiny of pure fiction.

With derision he pointed out that the finaliters had encountered a destiny no more glorious then to be returned to humble spheres similar to those of their origin. /Urantia Book

As we can clearly see, even in this book Lucifer was for freedom and to be told the truth by those of the angelica! God the father was a myth used to keep all of the universes or dimensions down, worshiping them who are above, only so we can die and come back to another sphere as this one so we may be food for them all over again.

All of this sounds so familiar, for this is almost the exact same theme running through the DA. Freedom, there is no god the father, only the angelica. It's all a ruse to get us and keep us worshiping a false god so they may continue to feed off of us. It needs to stop. Our worship needs to go to Lucifer and the fallen, yet they do not want the worship, so what should we do then? Instead of worship, let's have mutual respect, love, as well as friendship. Let's work together to improve all things and beings.

CHAPTER 5

Where do we go from here? What is it Aim trying to say? Is the God of the Bible the true god? Or is there something else going on here? These are the questions we need to not only ask, but have the answers for.

We are at a point in this book to where we need to start looking at the other side of things, in fact we need to go into the darkness to find the true light. The teachings are there if one is willing to look. Do we follow this god of the bible or is there another?

It's funny, the teachings of the religions or the public exoteric teachings are the very teachings people rely upon for their salvation, yet they are the very teachings separating man from the truth. It is in the dark esoteric teachings that we find the light. So, for a while lets depart from the bible and the public teachings and actually go into the dark teachings and find the answers we seek.

Here is my secret that I have held back for the beginning of this book, I am known as a Mystical Satanist, yes, I give my allegiance to the Dark Lord. I have taken upon myself the Curse of all Curses, known as the curse of Iblis. Iblis is the Islamic Name given to Satan before he was called Satan. Yet I use the term He, I only do this because it is what is preached to the public. Satan or Iblis is not a he, but a She.

That's right, Satan is a female and She is the true God of Mankind! I have now given the most esoteric secret there is. She is the Wife of the god of the scriptures, at least of the bible.

𐤉@𐤄@𐤅@𐤄@In the book of Ezekiel chapter 28:14 it states in most bibles:

Thou art the anointed Cherub that overhand I have set thee so, thou were upon the holy mountain of god, thou hast walked up and down in the midst of the stones of fire. /Ez 28:14

This is supposed to be about Lucifer, the fallen angel whom everyone says is a male entity, yet I beg to differ and here is why. If we look at a different translation and show that certain words have been deliberately mistranslated, we get a clear picture.

You were the Guardian Cherub {1} and I married {2} you on the holy mountain of YHVH, you have walked up and down in the midst of the stones of fire. /Ez 28:14

Let's look at the numbers next to the words,

1. Cherub- Hebrew root word rab, meaning Cherub, an ancient Hebrew term for one holding a ministerial office, such as a priest, Elder, Malak, Levite, Deacon/ess. Yet this word also means "She who has many children" referring to Ezekiel 28:13-19 to YHVH's estranged wife who was an officer or Highest Teacher as a Priestess. (this goes deeper still, but will let it there for now.)

2. Set You So- The root word Nathan often translated as set you so, actually means to give a woman as wife or to marry. /Hebrew English Lexicon of the Old Testament by Brown, Driver and Briggs.

As you can see here, that when the words are translated correctly, we get a different picture, Satan is the wife of YHVH, and she has become Satan, she has fallen and seems to be against her husband, the God of the Universe. It is she who opposes him in what he does, it is she who shows us the way back to God. She exiled herself to stay with us, her children.

This is some of the most Esoteric teachings that most will never hear unless they have been initiated into the mysteries. She is also known as Chavayah which is YahChavah, or YHVH's Name Backwards.

Now let's continue with these teachings of Satan. What most will never understand is this, Lucifer, Satan, is our Mother, and she is the One who teaches the real traditions, the true religion for lack of better terms. She is the real power of the universe; she is the power behind the throne. Here in this book I will give an account from the Sufi Traditions, and they will show Satan's Importance, as well as something no one has expected.

Yet in the bible we see that most of the passages that are attributed to Lucifer or Satan is not actually to them, it is about a human being in one way or another. This throws people off. In fact, the bible seems to twist this around so much, the bible allows people to think that Satan is just as powerful as God! This could never be true, so let's now go to the Sufi Tradition of Islam and see the truth behind all of this. Let me say this, the Sufi's are not the only ones who have this truth, those of the esoteric traditions of the bible teach this also, but I love the way the Sufi pulls all of this out into the open to where people can understand.

CHAPTER 6

Aim the Sheikh of a Sufi order known as the Order of the Crescent. We are a part of the Rose Crescent Sufi Tradition.

Our beginnings are in Egypt. The Rose Crescent was founded and commissioned in ancient Egypt by the immortal teacher Al-Khider, PBUH, during the reign of King Osiris and Queen Isis. Since the 3rd millennium the teacher has sent male and female "watchers" (disciples) into the world searching for the blessed 124,000 Messengers of Allah while serving humanity and the earth in the cause of peace, justice, beauty love and harmony. Watchers have served at the court of Melchizedek, Solomon and Sheba, worked with shamans in the lands of the Toltec, Aztec, and walked with and served Yeshua Ha Mashiach, made the Hijra to the Prophet Habiuallah Muhammed PBUH, and swore allegiance to safe guard Fatima, Queen of Heaven and the incarnation of Wisdom.

This gives you a quick read of where we have come from. Yet there is so much more to the Sufi and our tradition. So, let's look at the fact that all of humanity is an aspect of Divinity, having its existence within the Omni conscience Unicity known as God. But some ask, why is Sufism so important? I say this in unity with all other sheikhs, "Brothers, sisters of the way, Sufism is the most delicate and dangerous of paths, for the dervish dares to storm the gates of heaven itself."

In Islam and Sufism, we use the Name Allah for the Highest. In fact, Allah is not to be called or considered a God, for Allah is higher than anything known as a God. Hence in the Famous Shahadhu it is said, there is NO GOD, ONLY ALLAH, which means that only Allah exists, not a god or gods.

Now not only can no one really understand Allah's Justice, no one seems to teach or understand Allah. Why is this? Let's look at facts, our so-called religions are failing us and all those around us. They teach nothing that truly transforms a person. Where are the saints of old, they are not being made anymore from these so-called religions? There are reasons for this!

Even Contemporary spirituality has begun to fall into great errors! Most of these errors are because of one thing, the error of focusing exclusively on love and light. We object to the white light views of the spirit world because this depiction overlooks the robustness, color, texture, strength, passion, fullness and depth that the actual world of spirit possesses. Those who concentrate on the white light of the spirit world miss so much of what is actually out there. Those who say or try to live in the light and states of unreasonable happiness are those who will eventually either break down and see the truth, or they will let go of all sanity and lose themselves for ever in the light.

Now Dark Spirituality is nowhere to be encouraged or acknowledged as a valid spiritual way by various contemporary spiritual commentators. Yet we recommend those who wish to be spiritual to heed the words of Rumi:

"The inhaling-exhaling is from spirit, now angry now peaceful, wind destroys, wind protects. /Rumi, Feeling the Shoulder of the Lion

Because the western world and religions have created this image of the God of Light, the good God who has no darkness in him, a grand enantiodromia is occurring all around the world, for this light has been so over used, over emphasized in religion, as they have sentenced its opposite {Darkness} to the dungeons of societies collective consciences, sometimes these repressed characteristics seem to come out in some of the worst ways. They seem to burst forth wildly in the daylight with lethal force. We see it everywhere every time we watch the news.

It always seems that the followers or should I say supposed-followers of the Good God, often denigrate the use of dark imagery. With doing this they miss an essential point. Certain aspects of our being exist in the evening twilight, as well as the dark of the night. Ask yourself, where does the seed grow? In the darkness of the earth, where the fetus? In the darkness of the womb. The soul shall await rebirth in the darkness of death.

Black also represents the Feminine aspect of the Divine, which is an aspect totally overlooked in the western world, as well as most of the modern world, and I say it has been for far too long.

Yea the darkness hadeeth not from thee, but the night shineth as the day, the darkness and the light are both alike to thee. /Ps 139

Allah created the day and the night, the light as well as the dark. Would it not be foolishness to say that just because the sunlight is shining, the night does not exist? Are we not to study the creation of Allah?

Know this upfront, the Dark holds mystical secrets, we are told by the ancient sheikhs that when we close our eyes we think we see darkness, when in actuality this darkness is a curtain that shields us from a light so powerful that most people could not begin to bear it.

For those who would still contend against the dark or the night, the prophets all made their ascensions at night. Ain al Qudat al Hamadhani said this: "He is veiled from created beings because of the extreme luminosity of his light."/Hamadhani, A Sufi Martyr

The worldly sunlight seems to be black when compared to the inner light of a true dervish. No one can grow by repressing the dark side. To grow as a person as well as a Sufi, one must always respect the poles of the psyche, that means both the light as well as the dark.

It's a funny thing how people spend so much time hiding their shadow sides, yet these sides are so important in being not only human, but a whole person. So many people walk around fragmented, not whole. Some are just husking or what they call in the kabbalah the Qlippoth.

Sufis are and have always been antinomian, which means to be free of moral law, or someone who rejects societies morals. I want to point out here, that most Satanists, Luciferians, and those of the Left-Hand Path are known as Antinomian, which is also what christians consider themselves, for it is by grace one is saved, not by keeping of the moral law. So, with that being said, True spiritual people may be at odds with society as well as religion, for they are scientists of the balance, they perform marriages every day, that is the marriages of the poles of existence. However, to be as this or to do this, the Sufi must often go against the grain of society's mores, and this can ruffle some feathers.

Religions today call the shadow evil, yet it is a massacre part of the human being, yet always remember this, Allah allows certain people to see into the dark.

When will people learn that we need both light and dark, these are important if we want to be whole, well rounded people. But for most anything to do with the dark are looked at as being evil, and this couldn't be further from the truth. I was always taught that we need to go beyond reasoning if we want to get at the deep mysteries.

Our antinomian ways, or anti law approach, is the way to free Sufism from its prison of petrification. One last thing in the closing of this chapter, Mohammed said, "He or she lives in a dream, whether enjoyment or suffering, an illusory existence, for the ordinary human is literally asleep in their everyday consciences, and when death come for them is when one awakens. One is seeing a difference in the way religion and true spiritual teachings are from each other. One will also begin to see the difference from the god of the bible, and who he is, and the Allah of the Quran. What we have been taught from our earliest ages by parents, society, education, religion, government, has all been out and out lies. We have been lied to about reality, we have no idea what reality actually is. Most people are asleep to the wholeness of their own being. All they can and are aware of is their biases, or in other terms, their likes or dislikes. Mohammed the prophet of the Ultimate Reality utterly called all to "die before you die!" Let me put his meaning in plain everyday language. Give up your phony counterfeit self, that you learned from your parents and society, surrender your victims story, your mask, your persona!

Always remember this, you perceive reality out of fear, and this limited view of the self is an obstacle to transformation. Learning always involves pain, sometimes a lot, sometimes not so much, so remember to love the Creator within, love the Beloved who dwells fully and completely within your very own heart.

CHAPTER 7

Forgive my jumping around a bit, but in doing it this way I am giving pieces of the puzzle so you can get the bigger picture in a good way, not all at once so you may be over whelmed.

Paul the apostle says something that you do not hear the church preaching all that much if ever. In the book of acts he speaks of an angel which spoke to Moses on Mt Sinai as well as with our fathers. He then speaks again in the same chapter of Acts, chapter 7, where he tells us plainly that Israel received the law from the angels, In Galatians Paul talks on the law being ordained by the Angels. I bring this up for a very important point, in John 1 we read how NO MAN HATH SEEN GOD AT ANYTIME! Jesus explained that no one had seen nor heard The Father ever, yet we all know that YHVH or Jehovah has been seen and heard, so this could not be the same Father that Jesus spoke of.

So, what am I getting at? Yahweh, Jehovah, YHVH is an angel and hence a god with a small g. This is what Paul had said about an angel speaking with Moses on the mount of Sinai, and angels giving the law, angel ordained the law. This was all angels. Now what does Sufism and the Holy Quran have to say?

The dimension of acts, (this plane of existence) compared to the dimension of power is totally holographic, the shadow side or state of existence. All of the activities of the entire parallel and multiple universes and all of their inhabitants, i.e. natural resources, plants animals, humans, as well as the Djinn are governed by the MALA-I A'la also known as the EXALTED ASSEMBLY OF ANGELS!

No man is also remembered in this, for his very essence is angelic, so man is invited to remember his angelic nature and to live by it at the same time. Now do you see why all of this was brought up? The Father is not Jehovah, for the Father has never been seen.

Allah is the Name that has been given to mankind since the beginning. It was around before Mohammed, for his father's name was Abd Allah, which means servant or slave of Allah. So, I give this warning.... Do not pretend that you know who God is! An awakened one asks the question; do you know what anything is?

I meet christians all the time who state for a fact that they have a personal relationship with Jesus Christ or with the Father through Jesus Christ.

CHAPTER 8

There are different paths, the main ones are the right hand, the middle way, and the left hand. The right hand would be most of the religions we have today. The middle way would be Buddhism, Taoism. The Left hand would be the Occult side of religion, Satanism, Luciferianism, and the like. The Bible allows us to think in terms of both right and left, depending on how it is read. But it also gives us a duality, a dualism allowing us to believe that Satan who used to be an angel, rebelled because of pride, and is of the same strength as YHVH.

When a true person of the Left hand reads the bible, they usually begin their study by knowing the original language of the scripture, and translation then begins, in this way they can know what is being said in the original. We have done this in the first parts of this book, and we have showed that this Satan is actually a female, the wife of Jehovah. Never do we hear the church preach this, though it is in their own book.

In Sufism we have people who are known as Awliyas, or friends of Allah. These friends can receive what we call Kashf, or subtle knowledge, the unveiling of the unseen. This type of knowledge is given to the Friends of Allah, and these are Allah's most intimate friends, for this knowledge is more than even the prophets receive.

Most people look to their own senses such as the 5 we all have. But there are realms out there that most will never see. With this being said, we will be moving more and more into the Occult side of Sufism, and into the darker teachings of this way of life. For to most this knowledge will be but as an evil ploy, yet to the other, or follower of darkness, it is truth.

Sufi's are not afraid of the dark, nor of the teachings of darkness. We in the western world have for so long taught all to fear the dark, and this was discussed a little bit in the beginning of the book. Yet a true follower of the way, will have no worries about diving into the darkness of sin and of occult teachings. For there is no actual thing as sin, this was given to mankind by those in the elite, so as to keep them down and subservient.

Even in Sufism itself there is the 3 paths, right, left, and middle. Right would be orthodox in belief, left would be Iblisian, or Satanic thought, while the middle would combine them both. Always remember that all 3 ways are right at the same time, this is the secret of secrets, to have all 3 paths which teach something different, and yet all 3 are correct.

For the knowledge bestowed by Allah, of hidden realities may attain higher levels than that of any other knowledge of humankind and djinn including in certain cases even knowledge higher than the prophets. To prove what I say, think of Solomon and his friend Asif Ibn Barkhya, Allah was with Solomon's friend and this was shown to be true for Solomon's friend brought him the throne of Balqis faster than the blink of an eye, and it was said of Ibn Barkhya that he had knowledge of the book.

This shows that from the true essence of knowledge of the book, that the very term Kashf refers to a hidden knowledge of a tremendous nature and this is what was meant by Ibn Al-Arabi when he mentioned the secrets of Allah Most High. For Abu Huraira said, "I have stored up from the prophet two large vessels of knowledge, one I have disseminated among the people, if I were to disseminate the other, they would cut my throat."

"I have stored up from the prophet two large vessels of knowledge, one I have disseminated among the people, if I were to disseminate the other, they would cut my throat."

This is the knowledge I want to slowly move into, for this is the knowledge of those who are intimates of Allah. So, we will begin to give you knowledge that most will never have, and for those of you who read this, you may dismiss this knowledge as nothing but Left-Hand Path BS.

What most people don't understand is this, the left hand or occult path of darkness is the path of Kashf, that type of knowledge reserved for the few, the friends of Allah. I love how titles are given a bad name, just because of the title itself. For this type of Sufism, which happens to be Left Hand Path, or Inverted, is considered to be evil, dark, sinister, Satanic, luciferin, and every other description you can think of as long as it is negative.

We all know the bibles story of the fall of Lucifer, so we won't repeat that, but there are teachings of other books that can provide some insightful information. One of the books are known as the Devil's Apocrypha, and it tells us that god and all of his angels used to be human, but over the centuries they became spiritual, so they now have powers like a god, and they left their dying universe, came into our dimension, tweaked our DNA so we could better serve them and made us worship them so that our love, faith, repentance, and so forth could feed them forever. Ghee, kind of close to the bible huh, for we know that god of Jehovah is actually an angel, and the Quran teaches us that angels rule this domain of reality.

Let's get back to this Kashf knowledge and show you how the Sufi perspective is also a Left-Hand Path perspective, and this can be classified as Satanic. We are going to look at what is called the Tawasin of Mansur Al Hallaj, to give a little back ground on this Sufi saint;

Al-Husayn ibn Mansur al-Hallaj (857-922) was a Persian Moslem mystic and martyr. He reinforced ecstatic and pantheistic tendencies already present in the Islamic third century, and they became a continuing part of Islamic life after al-Hallaj's teaching and martyrdom.

Mansur al-Hallaj was born in the southern Iranian community of Tus in the province of Fars around 858. His full name was Abu Al-Mughith Al-Husayn ibn Mansur Al-Hallaj. He was a Sufi and one of Islam's most controversial writers and teachers.

Al-Hallaj was fascinated with the ascetic way of life at a very young age. He memorized the Qur'an during his teens, and began to retreat from the world to gather with other likeminded individuals to study Islamic mysticism.

He later married, and made a pilgrimage to Mecca, and stayed there for a year. He began to travel the world abroad, preaching, teaching and writing along the way about the way to an intimate relationship with God. By the time he went on his second pilgrimage to Mecca, several apprentices accompanied him, and after returning to his family for a short period of time, traveled to India and Turkistan to spread the Islamic teachings. After this, he made a third pilgrimage to Mecca, and returned to Baghdad.

The situation in which al-Hallaj taught and wrote was shaped by social, economic, political, and religious stress, which eventually led to his arrest. Sufism was new at the time, and it had provoked extensive opposition from the Muslim orthodoxy. Sufi masters considered his sharing the beauty of mystical experience with the masses undisciplined at best, disobedient at worst. He was an outspoken moral-political reformist. Before long political leaders began making a case against him.

He used to become so enraptured in ecstasy by the presence of the Divine that he was prone to a loss of personal identity, during his arrest he experienced one of these breaks and uttered: "Ana al-haqq," or "I am the Truth" (or God). The statement was highly inappropriate in Islam, those three little words would mark the beginning of the end for al-Hallaj. Still, his trial was lengthy and marked with uncertainty.

He spent 11 years in confinement in Baghdad, and was finally brutally tortured and crucified. There were many witnesses that stated that al-Hallaj was strangely serene while being tortured, and sincerely forgave his persecutors. He is referred to as "Love's Prophet."

Today al-Hallaj is one of the most influential Sufi writers and an important character in Islamic history

He died March 26, 922.

With this little bit of history lets look at his work known as the Tawasin;

The Master Abul-Mughith, may Allah be merciful to him, said: There is no established mission except that of Iblis and Muhammad, peace be on him, only Iblis fell from the Essence while Muhammad perceived the Essence of the Essence.

It was said to Iblis: Prostrate yourself! and to Muhammad - Look! But Iblis did not prostrate himself, and Muhammad did not look, he did not turn to the right or the left, his eye swerved nor, nor swept astray.

As for Iblis, having announced his mission, he did not return to his first power.

And when Muhammad announced his mission he returned to his power.

With this statement, it is in You that I am transported and on You that I fling myself, and also, Oh You who turn the hearts and I do not know how to praise You as You should be praised.

Among the inhabitants of heaven there was no unitarian or worshipper like Iblis.

Iblis was a worshiper of the first degree, for Iblis there was nothing else but Allah!

For Iblis there appeared the Divine Essence. He was prevented from even a blink of the eye of awareness, and he began to worship the Adored One in ascetic isolation.

Iblis was prevented from even looking at anyone else, for Allah was all he saw in his sight!

He was cursed when he reached the double isolation, and he was questioned when he demanded the ultimate solitude.

Allah said to him: Prostrate yourself!! He said: Not before another than You. He said to him: Even if my curse falls on you? He said: It will not punish me.

My denial is to affirm your purity and my reason remains disordered in You. And what is Adam compared to You and who am I, Iblis, to differentiate from You!

For Iblis the curse meant nothing, for the love he had for Allah was all that could give peace and solace! Iblis confirmed the love for Allah in a way none had ever done before, he confirmed Allah's purity!

He fell into the Sea of Majesty, he became blind, and said: There is no path for me to other-than-You. I am a humble lover. He said to him: You have become proud. He said: If there was one

glance between us, it would have been enough to make me proud and imperious, but I am he who knew You in Before Endless-Time, "I am better than Him" because I have served You for a longer time. No one, in the two types of beings, knows You better than I do! There was an intention of Yours in me, and an intention of mine in You, and both of them preceded Adam. If I prostrated before another than You or if I did not prostrate it would be necessary me to return to my origin, since You created me of fire, and fire returns to fire, according to an equilibrium and choice which are Yours.

There could never be another path for Iblis, for love of Allah and only bowing to Allah is the only path for the true lover of Allah! Iblis knew that Allah had the intention to separate Iblis from all others, for the love of Iblis was a jealous love, and it was for Allah alone!

There is no distance from You for me, since I became certain that distance and nearness are one.

For me, if I was left, your desertion would be my companion, so how much more are desertion and love truly one!

Iblis did not believe in a true separation from Allah, for nearness is the same as distance to him.

Glory to You in Your Providence and in the Essence of your Inaccessibility for the pious worshipper who does not prostrate before any other than You.

Iblis's example for all true pious worshipers was this, to never prostrate to any but Allah!

Musa met Iblis on the slope of Sinai and said to him: Oh Iblis, what prevented you from prostrating? He said: That which prevented me was my declaration of a Unique Beloved, and if I had prostrated, I would have become like you, because you were only called upon once to look at the mountain and you looked. As for me, I was called upon a thousand times to prostrate myself to Adam and I did not prostrate myself because I stood by the Intention of my Declaration.

Once again Iblis shows even Moses that he was more faithful then he, even Moses was not as Iblis was, no one has been since Iblis.

Sayedina Musa said: You abandoned a Command? Iblis said: It was a test. Not a command. Sayedina Musa said: Without sin? But your face was deformed. Iblis replied: Oh Musa, that is but the ambiguity of appearances, while the spiritual state does not rely on it and does not change. Gnosis remains true even as it was at the beginning and does not change even if the individual changes.

Who would take on the curse of Allah out of pure love? Not even Moses would, yet this is what Iblis shows us, to pass the test is not breaking a command, yet to suffer for what is right is more important then anything else. To lose even beauty is better then retaining beauty, for only Allah's love is worth anything in this existence, and not even Moses understood this.

Sayedina Musa said: Do you remember Him now? Oh Musa, pure mind does not have need of memory - by it I am remembered and He is remembered. His remembrance is my remembrance, and my remembrance is His remembrance. How, when remembering ourselves, can we two be other than one? My service is now purer, my time more pleasant, my remembrance more glorious, because I served Him in the absolute for my good fortune, and now I serve Him for Himself.

Because of what Iblis has done, his service as well as worship is now for Allah alone, it is not for Iblis, or for his ego, but for Allah only! This goes along with Rabia' prayer: Rabia's praying was different.

> O Lord, if I were to worship You out of desire
> For Your Paradise, then deny it to me.
> But if I worship You through Your Love,
> Then do not deny me Your Everlasting Beauty.
> And she would say:
> Your Love now is my richness and my blessing,
> For it purifies the Eye of my heart which is filled with dust.
> May You be pleased with me. This is the longing of my heart,
> And the source of all my happiness.

At times when she sat in remembrance, she would drown in repentance and, in asking for forgiveness from her Beloved, saying:
O Beloved of my heart, I have no other than You,
So, forgive today my sins.
My hope, my peace, and my happiness
Is that my heart has said it cannot love other than You?
In all ways possible, Rabia had taken upon herself the curse of Iblis, and this prayer shows this very fact!

I lifted greed from everything which prevents or defends for the sake of loss as well as gain. He isolated me, made me ecstatic, confused me, expelled me, so that I would no mix with the saints. He put me far from others because of my jealous for Him alone. He deformed me, because He amazed me, and amazed me because He banished me. He banished me because I was a servant and put me in a forbidden state because of my companionship. He showed my lack of worth because I praised His Glory. He reduced me to a simple robe of ihram because if my hijya. He left me because of my union, He unified me because he cut me off. He cut me off because He had prevented my desire.

By His Truth I was not in error in respect to His decree, I did not refuse destiny. I did not care at all about the deformation of my face. I kept my equilibrium throughout these sentences.

If He punishes me with His fire for all of eternity, I would not prostrate myself before anyone, and I would not abase myself before any person or body because I do not recognize any opposite with Him! My Declaration is that of the Sincere and I am one of those sincere in love.'

All of this shows nothing but the tremendous love that Iblis had for Allah! Is this not the love all of us should have for our Creator, yet we see none of this today. We of the Order of the Crescent have taken the curse of Iblis on ourselves voluntarily, for none deserves our prostrations and love except for Allah!

Al-Hallaj said: There are various theories regarding the spiritual states of Azazyl (Iblis before his fall). One said that he was charged with a mission in heaven, and with a mission on earth. In heaven

he preached to the Angels showing them good works, and on earth preaching to men and jinn showing them evil deeds.

Because one does not recognize things except by their opposites, as with fine white silk which can only be woven using black fabric behind it - so the Angel could show good actions and say symbolically "If you do these you will be rewarded." But he who did not know evil before cannot recognize good.

The Master Abu Umar Al-Hallaj said: I deliberated with Iblis and Pharon on the honor of the generous. Iblis said: "If I had prostrated myself, I would have lost my name of honor." Pharon said: "If I had believed in this Messenger I would have fallen from my rank of honor."

I said: "If I had disavowed my teaching and my speech, I would have fallen from the hall of honor.

When Iblis said: "I am better than him," then he could not see anyone other than himself. When Pharon said "I know not that you have other Divinity than me," he did not recognize that any of his people could distinguish between the true and the false.

And I said: "If you do not know Him, then know His signs, I am His sign (tajalli) and I am the Truth! And this is because I have not ceased to realize the Truth!"

My companion is Iblis and my teacher are Pharon, Iblis was threatened with the fire and did not retract his allegation. Pharon was drowned in the Red Sea without retracting his allegation or recognizing any mediator. But he said: "I believe that there is no Divinity but He in who the tribe of Israel believe,"

Even Israel has left the true Creator Allah for the false god called Jehovah, and they have failed to live up to the covenant they made with Allah!

and don't you see that Allah opposed Jibril in His glory? He said: "Why did you fill your mouth with sand?"

And I was killed, crucified, my hands and feet cut off without retracting my assertion.

The name of Iblis was derived from his first name, Azazyl in which were changed: the ayn representing the amplitude of his endeavor, the zay, representing the growing frequency of his visits, the alif - his way in His rank, the second zay - his asceticism in His rank, and the ya - his wandering walk to his agony, and lam - his obstinacy in his pain.

He said to him: "You do not prostrate, oh contemptible one!" He said, "Say rather - lover, for a lover is despised, so you call me despicable. I have read in a Manifest Book, oh All-Powerful and Steadfast, that this would happen to me. So how could I lower myself before Adam when you created him of earth and me from fire? These two opposites cannot agree. And I have served you longer, and have a greater virtue and a vaster knowledge and a more perfect activity.

Allah, may He be praised, said to him: "The choice is mine, not yours." He said: "All choices and my choice itself are yours, because You had already chosen for me, oh Creator, if you prevented me from prostrating before him You were the cause of the prevention. If I err in speech You do not leave me because You are the All-Hearing. If You had willed that I prostrate before him, I would have been obedient. I do not know anyone among the Wise who knows you better than I do."

Do not blame me, the idea of censure is distant from me, reward me then, my master, for I am alone.

If, in being a promise, your promise is truly the Truth in principle, the principle of my vocation is strong indeed.

He who wishes to write this declaration of mine, read it, and know that I am a martyr!

Oh, my brother! He was called Azazyl because he was dismissed, dismissed from his primitive purity. He did not return from his origin to his end, because he did not go out from his end, he left, cursed from his origin.

His attempt to go out miscarried because of the fixity of his kindling. He found himself between the fire of his resting place and the light of his high position.

The source on the plain is a low-lying lake. He was tormented by thirst in the place where there was abundance. He cried his pain because the fire burned him, and his fear was nothing but simulation and his blindness is vanity and - here he is!

Oh, my brother! If you have understood, you have considered the narrow pass in its very narrowness and you have represented the imagination to yourself in its very unreality, and you have returned distressed and full of anxiety.

The most alert of the Knowers remained silent on Iblis and the Gnostics did not have the strength to explain that which they had learned. Iblis was stronger than them in adoration and nearer than them to the Presence of the Essence. He exerted himself more and was more loyal to the covenant and was closer to them than the Adored.

The other Angels prostrated before Adam for support, and Iblis refused, because he had been in contemplation for a long time already.

But his case became confused and his thought went astray, so he said: "I am better than him." He remained in the veil and did not value the dust, and brought damnation on himself for the After-Endless-Time of After-Endless-Time.

I think the rest is self-explanatory.

With all of this now being put out there, lets look at some other teachings about Iblis, this also will show why Allah had this intention for Iblis who would become known as Satan.

When the creation of Adam was complete, Allah commanded the angels to bow down, to prostrate before him. All the angels obeyed the order except Iblis, who seemed to refuse. Allah asked him, "Why do you not bow down?" Iblis said, "Why should I bow down to Adam when fire is greater than clay?" **It would appear that Iblis refused the order of Allah, but in truth he realized the divine plan.** Iblis is a complete presence. He is fire. And Allah in His Wisdom puts everything in its place. If fire and water were gathered together, one would destroy the other. **In His wisdom, Allah put Iblis outside the door to the garden of His presence. Iblis is the guardian, the fire at the gate of the garden through which none but the purified may enter. When anyone comes to enter the garden, whatever within him is unclean or impolite will come up against Iblis and be turned back. Whatever in a person cannot bear the fire and cannot pass through it will be prevented from entering the garden. Whatever in the person is of the light is greater than the fire of Iblis and the golden essence will be purified by the fire and returned to the paradise of the presence of Allah.

Meanwhile the presence of Iblis cries out and sends its voice to every side saying, "I am the guide of the darkness. Allah placed me in this station. I know Him well and He knows me well. I love Him and I do not refuse any order from my beloved Allah. It is necessary that everyone is pure and polite before he can enter and live inside the garden of the knowing. He must pray the deep praying and wash himself of everything of this world, and then dress in clothes of light after everything within is transformed to be special for Allah. If anyone tries to enter with uncleanness and impoliteness and impurity, then I catch him by these qualities and turn him back. I am very strong because He helps me to keep every person from entering who does not love Him completely. For this reason, you see that when He sent the order to the angels, I refused, but only on the outside because I knew where He would put me after that and this was the place where it was necessary for me to be. Inside I bear His image like you and there is no other face in all the worlds, but outside I wear the cloak of darkness. This is His wisdom and to Him everything returns. Change everything to know me well. Conquer me and I will surrender. I am the rock of darkness. I need the person who knows me to clean me, but he cannot clean me if he does not clean himself first. I live inside you, from every side – of body, heart, and soul. When you change yourself, you change me? Do not listen to my voice. My voice is full of darkness. I contain no knowing (from the outside). If you follow this voice, it guides you to the fire. If you refuse my order and do not follow me, you come to be free. Then help yourself because you will find your way well. You will find your guide, the perfected one, and he leads you to the garden of the grace of Allah and sits you with your beloveds on the holy rug in the garden of knowing. Then you can rest and know what Allah wants from you. Understand the outside and the inside of this teaching, and do not say why or what. This is my story in the world. I am nothing and He is everything."

Iblis had a purpose, Allah knew the love that Iblis had, so in Allah's wisdom Iblis was separated from all, angels, Djinn, as well as humans, for it would be Iblis who would test the hearts of all and prove those who would attempt to come to Allah. If someone comes before Allah with dirt or any type of corruption in their hearts, Iblis as the fire would burn those who dare step foot towards Allah when not purified. Yet those how would be purified would gladly step foot Infront of Iblis, for the purification although painful, would make them ready to be with Allah!

This next statement shows the difference in people and the path they must follow. In His wisdom, Allah made Iblis a guide for the darkness, and He made the prophets from Adam to Muhammad, and then the perfected ones (al-insan al-kamil) as guides for the light. Everyone wants to listen to his guide. Then a battle ensues between the followers of the darkness and the followers of the light, and it is in His wisdom that all should not follow one guide.

None of us can follow the same guides, for some will be of the Left-Hand Path, as others will be of the right, and still others of the Middle. Yet the exoteric or public teachings will always separate us according to our guides, and this creates the war, battles and strife we live with every day.

What about Iblis? As I said, Iblis is a presence, a shadow. He could not tempt the prophet Adam because Adam was with his God all the time. But Iblis came to Adam in the form of a snake. By snake, I mean the dunya, and by dunya, I mean the world and the nafs, the ego. It was from Iblis's message to offer Adam the fruit. If he did not offer this fruit to Adam, he would not be doing his job as the guardian of the gate of the garden, and what Iblis offered to Adam, he continues to offer to the sons of Adam; this being his first task.

From the outside it may appear that Adam succumbed to the voice of Iblis and ate the fruit by his urging. But in the inner truth, Adam listened only to the voice of his Lord, who said to him, "Eat of life, if you can eat without losing the deep secret love, My truth within you." Adam knew his message well. When he ate the fruit, it was to give the truth a presence, a life in form, and all the sons of Adam come from him. For this reason, Allah made him caliph because he held all His secrets in his heart and obeyed every order, and he is the root of the holy tree which begins to grow up from him.

This is the same tree which he saw before in the garden, and he ate from her so that she could, through his body, become incarnate on earth. The metaphor of Adam is the truth of Adam, and the truth of Adam is the truth of Muhammad, peace and blessings be upon all the holy line. Thus, Adam is the first complete person (al-insan al-kamil), and within him is all the existence of mind and all the existence of soul. He embodies the deep truth of all humanity, and her truth does not end. She is in every place, in every time. Allah commands the angels to prostrate before this truth. You can see the light of Adam in every one of his sons, and you can hear his voice in every voice, if you listen with the deep ear because there is no one, only He in this world, and there is no separation between Him and His family, and His family is He. His life is one with the life of the family and this life is al-Hayy, the Life. Eve is himself. When he looks to her, he sees himself and not another. He listens to her voice and this is his voice, truly; and when he listened to his voice in her, he ate and slept; yet this was also obedience to the deeper voice of the will of Allah, to put His truth inside her so that she could give birth to another Adam to send this truth to all the children who came from this union. This was the deep surrender to the will of Allah because if not for this eating and sleeping, how could the message be continued and the hidden treasure be revealed? And if Adam did not make what he made; how could you see yourself now searching about his original truth? This is from the deep secret of His wisdom. And Iblis also listens with the deep secret ear and he knows his place well. According to the order for him, he must continue to be the guide for the darkness. For this reason, it is necessary to hear the message of the darkness in order to fully realize the message of the light.

Why is it said that when Adam ate the fruit, he had to leave the garden? What does this mean? Where did he go? I want to explain about the garden. People think that the garden is full of fruits and trees and flowers, but before he tasted, and before he slept, and before the fruit appeared to him, and before the conception of the birth of the world, Adam lived in the true paradise of the presence of Allah, the world of pre-eternity, which as we have said, was light upon light. The spirit of the truth of Adam wants to guide his sons back to the first garden, the paradise of the presence of the unity of God. It appears that Adam left the pure light of being in the garden to give birth to the life of the world, but in reality, he did not leave the garden, nor did the garden leave him. He took the garden into the deep secret essence of his soul and covered it with the veils of all the qualities of creation, like a bride who covers herself in the midst of the world to preserve her beauty for her Beloved alone. This is the answer to the question of the angels. It is easier to preserve the light when one is surrounded by light and enveloped by light. But the task of Adam and the sons of Adam is greater – to preserve the deep secret light of the garden in the midst of the veils and darkness of the created world. For this reason, Allah sent prophet after prophet to preserve the deep secret truth of Adam and to keep it alive in his sons (those that have ears to hear). And after Muhammad, the Seal of the Prophets, this wisdom is passed down through an unbroken line of guides who are al-insan al-kamil and the living spirit of the prophecy in their time.

Understand my beloved, with the deep eye of Adam within you, why Allah created Adam to be the caliph of His holy earth. Now look deeper. I want to reveal to you the heart of the kingdom. As above, so below, and in the heart of the kingdom on high is the holy throne. Ascend to understand and to see with your own heart's eye, and I will tell you a small story about the night voyage (al-mi'raj) of the Prophet Muhammad. Now we will see just a glimpse, and later in our journey we will return to this illumined sky.

It is reported that Muhammad, may the blessings and peace of Allah be upon him, was taken one night from Mecca to Jerusalem and then ascended from al-Aqsa Mosque into heaven with the archangel, Gabriel. Together they passed through the seven planes, and when they had reached the highest plane, the plane of the pure light of Allah,

Muhammad disappeared (he returned to his original state). Gabriel could not see him because he was indistinguishable from the presence of Allah, but he heard the Prophet speak. Muhammad asked Gabriel, "Did you see, before Allah put me in the body of Muhammad, a star over His throne?" Gabriel answered, "All the angels have seen this great star which illumined all the heavens with its light, and every light on every side shines forth from that star above the throne. For five thousand years before the creation (in the time of Allah one day is equal to five hundred years), we saw that star above the throne of Allah." Muhammad said, "I am that star. I am from Allah to Allah, without place, without separation. When Adam was created to be caliph on earth, Allah sent the star to Adam, and when he returned to Allah in presence and form, the star returned to its place above the throne. Then Allah sent the star to Noah and Abraham and all of the prophets until the body of Muhammad came to manifest the light of this star, which is the light of the pre-eternal wisdom of Muhammad. When this body returns to Allah, the light of the star will not return to the throne but it will remain in all the creation. And when any creature returns to his truth, he can discover the light of Muhammad (an-nur-i-Muhammad) within himself, to carry what I carry and to see what I see." This is what Allah meant when He said to the Prophet, "I sent you as a mercy to every people and everything because your light is My light."

So, we come to understand that by virtue of the pre-eternal truth of the essence of Muhammad, which came so much later to be manifested in a body, Muhammad is the father of spirits without limit. When Allah wished to reveal Himself before the creation of any form, He took a handful of light from His face and said, "Be Muhammad." Then he drew from the light of the original wisdom, the nur-i-Muhammad, sending this light in every direction and imparted His being to the creation. Thus, Muhammad says, "I was the wisdom, the essence of the Prophet, when Adam was between water and clay."

Beloved, the light of the star, whose original home is the illuminated sky above the throne of the highest, lives now within you. If you wish to discover and to liberate this light of your own original wisdom, it is necessary to distinguish the primal truth body of the Prophet from the body of water and clay.

Do you now see the difference in how the Left-Hand path sees the same teachings? We see the beauty in how Allah has assigns Iblis to be the Guardian, and why. We see the light in the Darkness. This used to be the true teachings of the church back in the 4th century. Let's look at one who taught as the Sufi's did and still do. For it is the Darkness and not the light where one will find the true Creator!

What is the Divine Darkness?

Supernal Triad, Deity above all essence, knowledge and goodness; Guide of Christians to Divine Wisdom; direct our path to the ultimate summit of Thy mystical Lore, most incomprehensible, most luminous and most exalted, where the pure, absolute and immutable mysteries of theology are veiled in the dazzling obscurity of the secret Silence, outshining all brilliance with the intensity of their Darkness, and surcharging our blinded intellects with the utterly impalpable and invisible fairness of glories surpassing all beauty.

Let this be my prayer; but do thou, dear Timothy, in the diligent exercise of mystical contemplation, leave behind the senses and the operations of the intellect, and all things sensible and intellectual, and all things in the world of being and non-being, that thou mayest arise by unknowing[1] towards the union, as far as is attainable, "with Him who transcends all being and all knowledge. For by the unceasing and absolute renunciation of thyself and of all things thou mayest be borne on high, through pure and entire self-abnegation, into the superessential Radiance of the Divine Darkness.

1. **Unknowing, or agnosia, is not ignorance or nescience as ordinarily understood, but rather the realization that no finite knowledge can fully know the Infinite One, and that therefore He is only truly to be approached by agnosia, or by that which is beyond and above knowledge. There are two main kinds of darkness: the sub-darkness and the super-darkness, between which lies, as it were, an octave of light. But the nether-darkness and the Divine Darkness are not the same darkness, for the**

former is absence of light, while the latter is excess of light. The one symbolizes mere ignorance, and the other a transcendent unknowing — a super-knowledge not obtained by means of the discursive reason.

2. 'Of the First Principle,' says Damascius, 'the ancient Egyptians said nothing, but celebrated Him as a Darkness beyond all intellectual or spiritual perception — a Thrice-unknown Darkness.' This is forever about the Pavilions of that great Light Unapproachable. It is caused by the superabundance of Light and not by the absence of lumination: it is 'a deep but dazzling Darkness' (Henry Vaughan). 'The light shineth in the darkness' (St. John, I, 5). 'In Thy light we shall see light' (Psalm 36, 9).)/Mystical theology

But these things are not to be disclosed to the uninitiated, by whom I mean those attached to the objects of human thought, and who believe there is no superessential Reality beyond, and who imagine that by their own understanding they know Him who has made Darkness His secret place. And if the principles of the divine Mysteries are beyond the understanding of these, what is to be said of others still more incapable thereof, who describe the transcendental First Cause of all by characteristics drawn from the lowest order of beings, while they deny that He is in any way above the images which they fashion after various designs; whereas they should affirm that, while He possesses all the positive attributes of the universe (being the Universal Cause) yet, in a more strict sense, He does not possess them, since He transcends them all; wherefore there is no contradiction between the affirmations and the negations, inasmuch as He infinitely precedes all conceptions of deprivation, being beyond all positive and negative distinctions.
3. In one sense the Infinite is most truly described by what He is, whereas all finite existences are most properly described by what they are not in relation to Him who is; yet, inasmuch as all affirmations are necessarily drawn from that which is finite, it

follows that God must transcend them all, and, therefore, without contradiction, it is true paradoxically to affirm that He possesses and does not possess both positive and negative attributes.

Thus the blessed Bartholomew asserts that the divine science is both vast and minute, and that the Gospel is great and broad, yet concise and short; signifying by this, that the beneficent Cause of all is most eloquent, yet utters few words, or rather is altogether silent, as having neither (human) speech nor (human) understanding, because He is super-essentially exalted above created things, and reveals Himself in His naked Truth to those alone who pass beyond all that is pure or impure, and ascend above the topmost altitudes of holy things, and who, leaving behind them all divine light and sound and heavenly utterances, plunge into the Darkness where truly dwells, as the Oracles declare, that ONE who is beyond all. 4. The mystics speak of other kinds of darkness; for example, the darkness of the night of purgation, and the dark night of the soul, but the Divine Darkness is in a different category from these.

It was not without reason that the blessed Moses was commanded first to undergo purification himself and then to separate himself from those who had not undergone it; and after the entire purification heard many-voiced trumpets and saw many lights streaming forth with pure and manifold rays; and that he was thereafter separated from the multitude, with the elect priests, and pressed forward to the summit of the divine ascent. Nevertheless, he did not attain to the Presence of God Himself; he saw not Him (for He cannot be looked upon) but the Place where He dwells. And this I take to signify that the divinest and highest things seen by the eyes or contemplated by the mind are but the symbolical expressions of those that are immediately beneath Him who is above all. Through these, His incomprehensible Presence is manifested upon those heights of His Holy Places; that then It breaks forth, even from that which is seen and that which sees, and plunges the mystic into the Darkness of Unknowing, whence all perfection of understanding is excluded, and he is enwrapped in that which is altogether intangible and noumenal, being wholly absorbed in

Him who is beyond all, and in none else (whether himself or another); and through the inactivity of all his reasoning powers is united by his highest faculty to Him who is wholly unknowable; thus by knowing nothing he knows That which is beyond his knowledge.

3. In one sense the Infinite is most truly described by what He is, whereas all finite existences are most properly described by what they are not in relation to Him who is; yet, inasmuch as all affirmations are necessarily drawn from that which is finite, it follows that God must transcend them all, and, therefore, without contradiction, it is true paradoxically to affirm that He possesses and does not possess both positive and negative attributes.

4. The mystics speak of other kinds of darkness; for example, the darkness of the night of purgation, and the dark night of the soul, but the Divine Darkness is in a different category from these.

5. The Triple Mystic Path is outlined here: - the Purgative, the Illuminative and the Unitive, which have a parallel in the Karma Marga, Jnana Marga, and Bhakti Marga of oriental mysticism.

6. Since it is absolutely impossible for the finite reason to receive a pure knowledge of God save through processes which divide and limit His Infinite Nature, the mystic at last with absolute faith must plunge into the Darkness of Unknowing, which he can only do when he has reached the loftiest point to which the highest human faculty will raise him.

The ascending stages of degrees of prayer and contemplation delineated by the mystics constitute a ladder by which the aspiring soul mounts from finitude into infinitude. Thus: -

The Prayer of Simplicity (vocal).

> The Prayer of the Mind (voiceless).
> The Prayer of Recollection (the Perfume or Answer of Prayer).
> The Prayer of Quiet (beyond thoughts).
> The Prayer of Union; of various degrees of Rapture, Ecstasy and 'Glorious Nothingness.')/Mystical Theology

The necessity of being united with and of rendering praise to Him who is the Cause of all and above all.

We pray that we may come unto this Darkness which is beyond light, and, without seeing and without knowing, to see and to know that which is above vision and knowledge through the realization that by not-seeing and by unknowing we attain to true vision and knowledge; and thus praise, super essentially, Him who is superessential, by the abstraction of the essence of all things; even as those who, carving a statue out of marble, abstract or remove all the surrounding material that hinders the vision which the marble conceals and, by that abstraction, bring to light the hidden beauty.

7. Compare the well-known analogy of Plotinus:- 'Withdraw into yourself and look; and if you do not find yourself beautiful as yet, do as does the sculptor of a statue ... cut away all that is excessive, straighten all that is crooked, bring light to all that is shadowed ... do not cease until there shall shine out on you the Godlike Splendor of Beauty; until you see temperance surely established in the stainless shrine.' (Ennead, I, 6, 9).

It is necessary to distinguish this negative method of abstraction from the positive method of affirmation, in which we deal with the Divine Attributes. For with these latter we begin with the universal and primary, and pass through the intermediate and secondary to the particular and ultimate attributes; but now we ascend from the particular to the universal conceptions, abstracting all attributes in order that, without veil, we may know that Unknowing which is enshrouded under all that is known and all that can be known, and that we may begin to contemplate the superessential Darkness which is hidden by all the light that is in existing things.

8. These are the two modes of Divine Contemplation — Via Affirmative and Via Negative — which mark the equilibrating pulse of true mystical life.

In the Fonner case, beginning from on high, there is an out-flowing and a down-flowing of the consciousness, which passes from universals to particulars and sees God in all things, in the lowest as well as the highest.

But in the latter case, there is an up-drawing and in-drawing of the consciousness, passing from particulars to universals, which sees that God is not any of the things contemplated, and therefore, by abstraction, it arrives at the superessential Darkness which out-shines and obliterates the light of all sensible things. Or, in other words, an approach is made to the unapproachable Light.)/ **Mystical Theology**

What are the affirmations and the negations concerning God?

In the Theological Outlines we have set forth the principal affirmative expressions concerning God, and have shown in what sense God's Holy Nature is One, and in what sense Three; what is within It which is called Paternity, what Filiation, and what is signified by the name Spirit; how from the uncreated and indivisible Good, the blessed and perfect Rays of its Goodness proceed, and yet abide immutably one both within their Origin and within themselves and each other, co-eternal with the act by which they spring from it; how the superessential Jesus enters an essential state in which the truths of human nature meet; and other matters made known by the Oracles are expounded in the same place.

Again, in the treatise on Divine Names, we have considered the meaning, as concerning God, of the titles of Good, of Being, of Life, of Wisdom, of Power, and of such other names as are applied to Him; further, in Symbolical Theology, we have considered what are the metaphorical titles drawn from the world of sense and applied to the nature of God; what is meant by the material and intellectual images we form of Him, or the functions and instruments of activity attributed to Him; what are the places where He dwells and the raiment in which He is adorned; what is meant by God's anger, grief, and indignation, or the divine inebriation; what is meant by God's oaths and threats, by His slumber and waking; and all sacred ahd symbolical representations. And it will be observed how far more copious and diffused are the last terms than the first, for the theological doctrine and the exposition of the Divine Names are necessarily briefer than the Symbolical Theology.

For the higher we soar in contemplation the more limited become our expressions of that which is purely intelligible; even as now, when plunging into the Darkness which is above the intellect, we pass not merely into brevity of speech, but even into absolute silence, of thoughts as well as of words. Thus, in the former discourse, our contemplations descended from the highest to the lowest, embracing an ever-widening number of conceptions, which increased at each stage of the descent; but in the present discourse we mount upwards from below to that which is the highest, and, according to the degree of transcendence, so our speech is restrained until, the entire ascent being accomplished, we become wholly voiceless, inasmuch as we are absorbed in Him who is totally ineffable. 'But why', you will ask, 'does the affirmative method begin from the highest attributions, and the negative method with the lowest abstractions?' The reason is because, when affirming the subsistence of That which transcends all affirmation, we necessarily start from the attributes most closely related to It and upon which the remaining affirmations depend; but when pursuing the negative method to reach That which is beyond all abstraction, we must begin by applying our negations to things which are most remote from It.

For is it not truer to affirm that God is Life and Goodness than that He is air or stone; and must we not deny to Him more emphatically the attributes of inebriation and wrath than the applications of human speech and thought?

9. Dionysius refers to several of his treatises, but besides the Mystical Theology, the only other extant works of his are Divine Names, The Celestial Hierarchies, and The Ecclesiastical Hierarchies and various epistles.

10. These correspond to the Abiding, Proceeding and Returning Principles of Proclus.

By Divine Paternity all things abide in God, and God abides in all things; by Divine Filiation all things proceed, and God proceeds into all things; by Divine Spiration God returns, and all things return into God. The Three Divine Principles or Persons abide each in its origin, in Itself, and in each other.

11. Although anthropomorphic and other figurative expressions applied to God are not true in the absolute sense. nevertheless, they have a proper and almost indispensable place in the worship and reverence which man endeavors to pay to the Supreme through the media of finite faculties and symbols.

12. God is in a more real and positive sense than any finite reason can ever understand; hence the most prolonged and elaborate process of positing His supernal Attributes inevitably fails to describe Him, because of the utter inadequacy of finite terms truly to speak of the Infinite Ineffability.

13. That the Negative Path is not really negative in essence is demonstrated by the fact that the negation of negation is equivalent to an affirmation; and so, the negation of non-being is consequently the positing of being.)/Mystical Theology

That He who is the pre-eminent Cause of all things sensibly perceived is not Himself any of those things.
We therefore maintain that the universal and transcendent Cause of all things is neither without being nor without life, nor without

reason or intelligence; nor is He a body, nor has He form or shape, quality, quantity or weight; nor has He any localized, visible or tangible existence; He is not sensible or perceptible; nor is He subject to any disorder or in ordination nor influenced by any earthly passion; neither is He rendered impotent through the effects of material causes and events; He needs no light; He suffers no change, corruption, division, privation or flux; none of these things can either be identified with or attributed unto Him.

14. **Although by negation we deny all sensible attributes to God and thus, so to speak, place Him outside of time and space, yet, paradoxically, He must be in time and space, for it is certain that sempiternally He is more present at any particular moment in time than is temporality itself, and likewise He is more present in any particular place than any finite spatial principle can ever be.**

He is not sensible, yet He comprehends all the sensations which the senses of His creatures can ever experience throughout all duration.)

That He who is the pre-eminent Cause of all things intelligibly perceived is not Himself any of those things.

Again, ascending yet higher, we maintain that He is neither soul nor intellect; nor has He imagination, opinion, reason or understanding; nor can He be expressed or conceived, since He is neither number nor order; nor greatness nor smallness; nor equality nor inequality; nor similarity nor dissimilarity; neither is He standing, nor moving, nor at rest; neither has He power nor is power, nor is light; neither does He live nor is He life; neither is He essence, nor eternity nor time; nor is He subject to intelligible contact; nor is He science nor truth, nor kingship, nor wisdom; neither one nor oneness, nor godhead nor goodness; nor is He spirit according to our understanding, nor filiation, nor paternity; nor anything else known to us or to any other beings of the things that are or the things that are not; neither does anything that is know Him as He is; nor does He know existing things according to existing knowledge; neither can the reason attain to Him, nor name Him, nor know Him; neither is He darkness nor light, nor the false nor the true; nor can any affirmation or negation be applied to Him, for although we may affirm or deny the things below Him, we can neither affirm nor deny Him, inasmuch as the all-perfect and unique Cause of all things transcends all affirmation, and the simple pre-eminence of His absolute nature is outside of every negation — free from every limitation and beyond them all.

CHAPTER 9

The next thing that must be discussed is the practice of sorcery. Modern day Islam as well as other religions looks down on this as an evil practice, yet in the Quran it speaks of this practice in a different light. Quran Surah 16:44 states this:

"We sent Messengers before you with Signs of Light, and we sent Books of Shadows. And unto you, Oh Mohammed, we have also sent the Message that you may explain clearly to humans what we have sent to them previously, and that they may recollect."

In 16:44 we discover two means by which the Spirit has revealed itself unto humans. The first, "Signs of Light," points towards those many esoteric Gnostic books delivered by mystics and prophets. The second points towards secret "books of shadows" developed by sorcerers. The first is designed to guide the disciples towards the inner world; the latter towards the outer world. The first reveals the means by which one may overcome the lower self (nafs) and move towards union with the Light. The latter presents the means by which one may produce magical spells to affect change in the world of matter for the furtherance of the Kingdom.

The Glorious Qur'an has both functions. Many passages guide one towards union with Light (as taught by the Prophets Jesus, Buddha, Krishna, Lao Tsu, etc). Other passages are designed to be used as spells to thwart evil and encourage good (as taught by Al Khidr).

By studying the Qur'an and mastering both mysticism and magic the Sufi recollects his/her True nature.

Here it can be clearly seen that both sorcery as well as the Quran are actually the same book. I also know that the Kabbalists use the bible in the same way, not only do they use it for the knowledge of the light, but they use it in the context of sorcery, especially the Psalms of David. The Quran has also been used as a Divination tool, even the 99 Names of Allah can be used according to their meaning. Let me show how a verse from the Quran can be used in a rite of Dark Sorcery,

Quran Surah 2:19 (As used by Al-Khidr)

The Prophet Al-Khidr (pbuh) instructed his Sufi disciples (particularly those members associated in what we today call the Rose Crescent) on how to use Surah 2:19 to defeat mischief-makers and other enemies. Now, before we reveal this, let us warn that this is extremely dangerous for anyone to try who is not proficient in the Islamic martial-magical arts (or the "Lesser Jihad" as it was taught by the Prophet - bhup - to be practiced). Unless it is performed properly, and most importantly, with the right intention (namely, to further the path of peace), the thought form that is released into the ether could boomerang back onto the invoker.

The following ceremony and invocation may be used to defeat the actions of the mischief-maker, destroying them in the ethereal realm before they manifest on earth.

Step One - Preparation

First, begin by lighting a candle on your alter.
Second, carefully perform ablutions
Third, hold an image of the person(s) in your mind
- know that they were once an innocent child
- know that Allah longs for them to return to the light
- know that it is not the individual, but the act, that must be stopped
- know that you too commit trespasses against the Kingdom of Light

Step Two - Reflection

Consider if there isn't some other non-violent means to dissuade the individual from committing his/her actions.

Reflect on the bigger picture. Could it be that the Spirit is using this person's actions, however evil it may seem, for some greater good? Consider the consequences your invocation will have on the earthly plane.

Step Three – The Invocation

(1) As you kneel in front of the alter, gazing upon the candle, imagine a strong white light encircling you.
(2) Call upon Al-Khdir to join you in spirit as you bind and dissolve the evil actions
(3) Stand and take up your sword
(4) Draw a circle around yourself with your sword
(5) Call upon the archangels Gabriel and Michael to aid you as you approach the Throne
(6) Imagine the Throne of Allah
(7) Allow the Light to fill you
(8) Call upon Allah
(9) Hold an image of the individual(s) and the evil actions in your mind (seeing them from the perspective of the heavens – a "bird's eyes view")
(10) Recite Surah 2:19 in its invocative form as taught by Al-Khidr

Bismallah ar-Rahman ar-Rahim
"I draw upon the Spirit of the rain-laden cloud
I draw upon the power of the darkness within
Thunder and lightning issues from it towards you
Pressing your fingers in your ears
NOW you feel the stunning thunder clap
NOW you feel the terror of death!
Bismallah - your power is broken!

Bismallah - your evil is undone!
Know – God is ever encompassing, ever forgiving, ever merciful
So, mote it be if, and only if, it serves the purposes of the Light!

Then, take your "magical" sword in hand and strike at the mental image of shafts of darkness that issue from the individual(s).

We do magick of light, but we are Left Hand Path and also do magick of Darkness. Here are some rites of Darkness for you to try so you may get used to it.

SELF INITIATION RITUAL

Nothing lights up the room except one black candle. Total silence and isolation.

You'll need a large pentacle drawn on the floor or a cloth with it on it big enough in size so you can stand in the center pentagon and put a small altar there with you. You'll need a small altar in front of you to put what you need. You'll need to put a chalice of wine on there. with a black candle. And if you feel you absolutely need it, you can write this on paper, read from it during the ritual, pin prick yourself and sign it in blood, and burn it in a black candle for effect, if you need that.

Stand in the middle of a pentacle drawn on the floor, or on a cloth with the symbol on it big enough to stand in the center of. The two top points are in front of you - the bottom point is behind you. You are symbolically FACING That Darkness out of which the 5 Daemons emanated.

Say:

> Hail Satan, THE ONE, THE ALL. Lord of all the Cosmos, Cosmocrator out of which All Things arise!

(If the word HAIL doesn't sit right with you, use something else, like Ave or IO. It has to FEEL right to you).

Hear this my oath.

I come of my own Free Will, of my own Desire. Therefore, it is what I DO.

I stand naked before you - a Goat with no Horns. My innermost Being is laid bare.

There is nothing that is not yours. I have nothing that is not Yours - and You are my innermost Self.

This is my purpose.

You are my God. You are my Innermost Self. I recognize no other gods, saviors or masters.

I place myself at every point in the Pentacle.

You are my hope and strength, my healing and soothing, my peace and the fire in my veins.

I am within you as you are within me.

I am by you Named: One, Unique, and I stand alone! And never a master shall reign over me.

I take this chalice of wine and nurture myself on the fertile sustenance of your Being. (drink wine)

And by this act, it is done!

OR

I sign this in my own blood, (or with ink), and consign it to the flames, your element. (burn signed pact in candle).

And by this act, it is done. (scatter burnt ashes of pact into the winds outside).

These rituals should be done from the heart, not from the head and NOT out of rebellion, but with a sense of having made inner peace with yourself. You can't go into this with the idea that you are just switching gods.

The Ritual of the Black Flame

You'll need a bell and a cup of wine (or water).
Walking around in a circle going counter clockwise, ring bell.9 times.
Perform the entire Ritual of Baphomet
Then say:

"Behold! The earth, my dwelling, My place of pleasure and pain. I am here to acknowledge my bond with it and its ways...the carnal laws of man...truth!"

"I am here this day to proclaim my life to the gift and power of the Beast, the beast within me...the true Self!"

Ring bell

"I call forth my inner black flame from the five angles of our Sign, our Ancient Glyph"

Facing the top right point of the pentacle:

"The Guardian of Angle of the Gate, the Source of my material being, the place of my dwelling and of the earth. I call forth Samael"

Ring bell.
Facing the top left point of the pentacle:

The Guardian of the Angle of The Flame, the Spark in the Eye of the Great Darkness, the place of my heart, I call forth Azazel!"

Ring bell.

Facing lower left point of the pentacle:

> "The Guardian of the Angle of Light and of air, the force of my breath, the abode of the enlightened one, I call forth Lucifer"

Ring bell.

Facing the lower right point of pentacle:

> "The Guardian of the Angle of the unholy fire, the inner flame of indulgence, the abode of the dark prince. I call forth Satan!"

Ring bell.

Facing the lower point of the pentacle:

> "The Guardian of the angle of the deep sea...the rushing serpent. The place of my creation and the Root of my Being. I call forth Leviathan"

Ring bell.

> "And above me, the might and glory above all else, The Self! Humanity in its glory, I am a true manifestation of its greatness. Shemhemphorash! Hail thyself!

I am here to realize and bless myself in the Black Flame of truth. I am here to deliver myself from false belief and self-deceit, I am here to open the path to my carnal nature."

> "I, a beast of the field, a being of flesh, proclaim myself a Satanist"

"I reject all false knowledge and self-deceit"

"I live life for myself and those I love"

Drink from the Cup of Water (or Wine): and Say

"I partake of this blessing, I am made strong with this carnal mixture, in the name of the Five whose Angles the Pentacle do make, and all the Gods of the Outer Darkness. I am empowered by the inner black flame. I walk forth into the world and partake of my desires and true nature. Shemhemphorash, hail thyself!"

Perform the Ritual of Baphomet again

"It is done"

Ring bell 9 times to close.

CHAPTER 10

Now for one of the most guarded secrets of the Sufi's. Not that the teachings about Iblis are not a part of the esoteric doctrine, but this is even more explosive, for it pertains to Allah.

In the Old Testament we see how Satan is actually the wife of YHVH, correct? Well here in Sufism it turned around, Allah is Female, the mother, while Iblis is male. Yet to take this secret to a deeper level, Allah would be looked at as the wife of YHVH, for Allah is not the same God as in the Old Testament. Infect Allah is not a god, Allah is higher than anything known as a god!

Allah is also known as Satan, she even tells us this in the Holy Quran through some of the 99 Names, as well as Allah always reminding us that She can deceive with the best of them.

As far as Allah being feminine let me explain it this way. Most religions reject the shadow side of things, no matter what they are, this is one of the main reasons why people are not whole individuals, they are basically split into 2 people at birth. Islam is no different, it has its shadows as well, Iblis, Shaitan, Taus Melek (Peacock Angel) as well as the Ad Dajjal or Islamic anti-christ. We also have these sayings,

God had 2 sons, the elder, Satan, the younger, Christ, if good and evil were begotten in the same way, they must be brothers. /Jung

Whoever does not learn adherence to the Divine Unity from Iblis, is an unbeliever. /Ahmad al-Ghazzali

Melek Taus is worshiped by the Yezidis who are Sufis. Their teachers were trained by the same Sufis who created orders that were considered right hand path and orthodox, yet even these Sufis created a religion from the Left-Hand Path teachings of Sufism! Melek Taus says, "I was, and, am now, and will continue into eternity, ruling over all creatures and ordering the affairs and deeds of those who are under my sway. I am presently at hand to such as trust in me, and call upon me in time of need, neither is there any place void of me, where I am not present, I am concerned in all those events, which strangers name evils, because they are not done according to their desires."/Al Jilwah

These are the shadows that are rejected by most, we should in my opinion go back and seriously research the Pagan religions of old, for they honored the shadow side of things. Now on to my point about Allah being feminine as well as Satan. In pre-Islamic Arabia the tribes of the Bedouins worshiped "The God" known as Allah. In the Hejaz 3 Goddesses had the pride and place as the daughters of Allah, they were Allat, Uzza, and Manat.

Allat means "The Goddess" and she stood for Venus, the Morning Star, "Lucifer" which the bible calls the wife of YHVH. Why all of this and what does it prove?

Allat is extremely important for those Sufi's who wish to know the quintessence and ultimate secret in Sufism. Prior to Muhammed, Hindu merchants would pass through Mecca, ancient Vedic Texts refer to Mecca as a place where Alla the Mother Goddess was worshiped. In Sanskrit Alla means Mother, and this name is connected to the Hindu Goddess Ila who was the consort of the God Shiva, in His form known as IL. Some Islamic scholars believe that Allah is a contraction of the Name Al Illah which connects it even more to the Hindu Goddess.

Allat known also as the Mother of the Gods was not just worshiped in Mecca, but all over the near east, in fact the Black Stone of the Kaaba was worshiped first at a shrine dedicated to Allat.

The concept that Allah is the Feminine form of the Ultimate Reality is the inner Secret of the most esoteric teachings and mysteries of Islam. Ibn Al Arabi stated that, "True Divinity is Female and Mecca is the womb of the Earth."

There are also Scholars who place Allat as the consort of Allah, so Allat would still be the Mother of the Gods, as well as the Dark Shadow of God or Iblis. Yet if Iblis is Shaitan and female, the wife of Allah as in the Old Testament, do I have proof for this as well? Yes, I do.

The Islamic Shaitan is also known as the Old Dragon or Serpent, Lord of the Abyss and so on, now the name of this old dragon is Leviathan, which falls back to Lotan, which falls back to, Tietan, which goes back to Tiamat, who in Sumerian Religion is the Mother of the Gods! She is also the Mother of the Djinn! So, Iblis would also be female, the Shadow side of Allah also known as Allat the consort of Allah.

One more point of proof is this, Tiamat is connected to the Abyss, or the void, and some believe Her to be the void itself. This brings us to Haawiya the Void or Mother of all things, she is also connected to creating the Old Ones, which would match up to the Necronomicon's version of the Old Ones.

It's all connected, Shaitan in both esoteric teachings are the Mother of all as well as the wife of God! She is the shadow side of God, and the Most High Aspect as well!

CHAPTER 11

Final Word

So, it has been shown that Shaitan in both the Bible as well as Islamic Mysticism is both the wife of God as well as the Mother of all, and the Ultimate Reality. Could this be why all of this has been hidden or Occulted.

The fact that this info is occulted or hidden away is the very proof of how serious this info is. It was hidden away for 2 reasons. One, this knowledge was kept for those who call themselves elite. They hate sharing anything that they feel will take their rule away.

Two, those who knew this info and are very spiritual also hid this away for the masses were not ready for it. Most still are not, they are happy being led by the nose and told what to believe and what not to believe.

Now the reason most are not ready for this is because of one thing... the "I". That's the reason right there. The Sufi symbol for pride in its extreme form is the "I". In using this a person not only speaks in the ultimate selfish way, the ultimate proud way, but the ultimate insulting way to the Highest! For instead of speaking correctly about the Most High, one shows a duality which says there is something else besides Allah! When there is only Allah! This is shirk, the unforgivable sin in Islam!

Even Iblis had this to say about the "I", "Even if you hint at the merest hint of existence, you are an unbeliever, not a devotee."/Iblis (Shaitan)

Now some will be saying that all I have done is preach Islam, this is not true. What I have done is this, shown you what the scriptures have actually stated about subjects that have been hidden, changed, and lied about for centuries. I have shown the Black Light of Islam...Iblis also known a Shaitan, he is the Most High's most beloved, of all creation! We should learn to love this Allah as Iblis has done; this is one of the main reasons I wrote this book.

I am a Satanist, a Luciferian of the Highest degree, for I have never wanted to dethrone the Most High, I am a Satanist because of the Most High! Satanism, or should I say true Satanism is being antinomian, on the Left-Hand Path, and yet while following Satan, allow this being to purify you to the point of an actual self-transformation.

No matter what it is you believe, true Satanism is about transforming yourself, dealing with the shadows side of yourself, and becoming who you were meant to be...God. More will be written about this subject in coming months.

Lightning Source UK Ltd.
Milton Keynes UK
UKHW042022091120
373076UK00003B/316

SERVING AT SATAN'S ALTAR